*To Sarah, whose energy
and heart
never cease to inspire*

*Savoring the Shore may be purchased through our web site,* **www.savoringtheshore.com**
*Amazon.com and other retail outlets*
*Kindle and other devices*

*Is a community cookbook compiled by Cheryl Larkin and Kate Kurelja*

*Proceeds from this cookbook will benefit projects at the New Jersey Shore in response to the devastation caused by Hurricane Sandy.*

*The Savoring the Shore Project*
*Savoring Life, Inc.*
*96 Ford Road, Suite 15*
*Denville, NJ 07834*
**www.savoringtheshore.com**

# Because Every Little Bit Helps...

## Savoring the Shore

### How a couple of foodies got to rub elbows with some celebrity chefs and home cooks – and publish their recipes

We had no power for days after Hurricane Sandy and the strangest thing was not having access to media. We couldn't hear them telling our story. No Brian Williams or Diane Sawyer or George or Matt or Charlie to tell us how the shore had fared. No knowledge that Bruce and Jon were about to host a telethon to help. Around us on all sides were fallen trees and tangled wires everywhere. We finally heard Governor Christie on a car radio. The shore as we know it is gone he said.

Hurricane Sandy hit on Monday night and we were allowed back into the shore on Thursday morning. We did not have to take off work, there wasn't any. Life was subsistence – keeping what food you had cold, keeping yourselves and the baby warm, cooking at Kate's where she has a gas stove and showering at our house where we have a gas water heater. It sounds kind of cushy until you realize that the room temperature is plunging down daily to an ultimate low of 40 degrees F. We had about a tank of gas in one vehicle, enough to do a roundtrip to the shore.

The good news for us personally was that our cottage was spared. There were a few exterior things of course that were remedied in a couple of visits. We were so incredibly lucky. The bad news was that now we got to see the devastation that the power outages had shielded from us. Broken, crumpled buildings stood or half stood or were washed away. Sand dunes were re-created in the streets where we scaled them to survey the damage. Wires were down. Garbage and debris were scattered everywhere and seagulls patrolled what was left of sidewalks and driveways as Mother Nature's clean-up crew. The boardwalk was gone.

### So what do you do to help?

Like so many others, we shoveled a lot of sand, pulled down a lot of damage and bagged up a lot of debris. And, back home in north central NJ Kate and I both with full-time careers in the marketing world, talked about a cooking-related project we've been contemplating. As the baby cooed in her inclined chair the obvious hit us,

let's do a cookbook to fundraise for NJ Sandy relief. From there our food blog **www.savoringtheshore.com** was launched and along with help from daughter/sister Sarah (who is a graduate student at Rutgers and a terrific networker) we were on our way.

The purpose of Savoring the Shore has always been to celebrate the NJ shore in its various nuances. For in the heart of shore lovers' memories and traditions comes the strength to rebuild. If that sounds dramatic all of these months later, the truth is that there are still families as of this writing who are dealing with the devastation. Yes, the shore is open and it truly is wonderful, but there are also still many businesses from bakeries to bait shops to restaurants unable to reopen because of the gap between the insurance they might have had and the cost to restore and replenish the shelves. And there are still many, many families who are displaced. These are the whys of Savoring the Shore. The funds raised by the book will be directed to people such as these.

The chefs became involved thanks to a combination of old fashioned marketing and social networking, much of it via Facebook and Twitter. We have been humbled by the generous spirits of so many of the chefs and their immediate openness to participate. Chopped champion Chef Eric LeVine, who is a NJ restaurateur, is one of the chefs who follows and interacts with us on Facebook. He is a five time cancer survivor and no stranger to philanthropy. We met Chef LeVine through Savoring the Shore and he has two recipes in the book, one of which is Peanut Butter Mousse, Chocolate Mousse with Hazelnut Sauce. That pretty much says it all.

Facebook also connected us with the owners of Mueller's Bakery in Bay Head, NJ, a place we visit every weekend in the summer for good coffee and more pastries, breads and cakes than you could ever imagine. Mueller's was gutted by Sandy. Kate and I were honored when they took a few minutes in the midst of their reconstruction nightmare to share a recipe for Sour Cream Coffee Cake with Savoring the Shore.

Another Facebook discovery is the group Stars of Hope. They started in Texas and have spread across the country. Since Sandy they have founded a NJ chapter also. They gather children to make art projects – decorated stars – which are then mounted in devastated areas to remind victims to hold on to hope. It is so wonderful to think of how these children must feel when helping and how the recipients feel upon seeing their artwork. We know how good we feel that they have designed a Star of Hope just for Savoring the Shore. It and the Stars of Hope recipe for Zuppa de Pesce both appear in the book.

Another touching contribution has come from Mary's Place by the Sea in Ocean Grove, NJ, a sanctuary for women who are grappling with cancer. The center provides these women with rooms, person- alized meals, physical and emotional support and a place to rest and heal. We love that their nutritionist Linda M. Jensen has submitted a recipe for Choco Avo Mousse made with carob powder, avocado, almond butter and agave nectar.

Certainly our most educational Facebook connection has been Karen L. Schnitzspahn, author of nine books about NJ including her most recent, **Jersey Shore Food History Victorian Feasts to Boardwalk Treats.** The book is filled with information about the way the NJ shore has eaten through history and the food establishments that have spanned generations, some still operating today. It turns out the shore eateries served farm and sea to table years before our current reemphasis. This wholesome food, along with the ocean and fresh sea air, were what drew visitors to the NJ shore to refresh and restore. The new restaurant culture is reinvigo- rating this (think Chef David Burke's Fromagerie in Rumson and Chef Anthony Micari at The Ebbitt Room, Cape May). We reached out through Facebook to Karen and she has mentored us since. She also has submitted a delicious recipe for Fried Oysters on Toast with a bit of history on the side.

In terms of engaging with celebrity chefs, we owe much to Twitter including recipes that came in from Top Chef Masters Chef David Burke (Grilled Whole Salmon with Grilled Vegetables), four chefs from Hell's Kitchen Season 11 and one from Season 10 (Barret Beyer, Jessica Lewis, Amanda Giblin, Jacqueline Baldassari, and Justin Antiorio), and cookbook authors such as Louisa Shafia, **The Persian Kitchen,** who submitted Borani esfenaj (Yogurt with Spinach, Oregano, and Garlic) a lovely condiment for a range of dishes. A great favorite who has contributed a recipe is Chef Michel Richard, the James Beard Award winning chef who also appeared in two television episodes with Julia Child. He is in the process of opening a café and two restaurants in Manhattan. His contribution is Cherry Clafoutis, a delicious dessert. He is also a painter, and we are honored that he has contributed a sketch and a painting as well as a photograph of the dessert to Savoring the Shore.

We also have been fortunate to encounter several celebrity chefs in person. A recent fundraiser hosted by our friend Marguerite D'Aloia in Manhattan brought us face to face with Top Chef judge Tom Colicchio, which in the new world order of chefs as rock stars is akin to meeting Paul McCartney or Jon Bon Jovi. Since we are foodies we knew that Chef Colicchio is originally from NJ (which is not at all essential to our cause but helpful nonetheless). We are honored that he has shared his grandmother's delicious chicken soup recipe which is a memory from his growing up years.

Still others who have contributed are award winning NJ chefs and restaurateurs including several who made the Best Chefs America 2013 list: Chef Marilyn Schlossbach who owns restaurants in Asbury Park and Normandy Beach, several of which were badly damaged by Sandy, and Chef Mike Jurusz of Chef Mike's ABG (Atlantic Bar and Grill) in Seaside Park who has shared a recipe for Fresh Shucked Oysters with Bloody Mary Granite which taste like fresh sea air with a kick. Then there's Chef Drew Araneo of Drew's Bayshore Bistro in Keyport, which had to relocate because of Sandy. Chef Drew has submitted four recipes to Savoring the Shore. PS he also recently defeated Chef Bobby Flay in a Throwdown in Keyport. Shore lovers will also recognize Chef Joe Introne of Joe Leone's of Point Pleasant Beach and Sea Girt, who helped to launch us within the chef community by sharing our recipe submission form with his friends and employees. He has contributed two recipes to the book, St. Joseph's Day Pastry and Insalata di Arance featuring blood oranges, red onion, arugula and black olives. Joe Leone's is a favorite stop in our shore travels and all we can say is Yum!

In all there are 150+ recipes from chefs and home cooks in Savoring the Shore plus photos and stories, every one with a special memory for Kate and me. We are thankful to every single one who has submitted and to our wonderfully supportive families who've taste-tested the recipes along the way. Thank you too to our longtime friends and collaborators Bill and Susi Sahlman of Sahlman Art Studio, Inc. for so artfully arranging the recipes and shore stories into the finished book.

And since we are often asked, the recipe I have used almost weekly since Kate's and my original test of it is the first one that came in, Nancy's Fish to Shore (pun intended). It was submitted by longtime friend and extraordinary high school English and International Baccalaureate teacher Lucia Abercrombie Harvilchuck. Lucia at one time lived on a boat at the shore while teaching at Kent Place School in Summit. With a touch of seasoning and a sprinkling of freshly crushed crackers, her white fish recipe comes out perfectly every time. We hope that you will try it!

With gratitude,

Cheryl and Kate

4

# Table of Contents

Point Pleasant Beach, NJ

# Breakfast, Brunch and Breads

# Blue Cheese, Bacon and Herb Soufflé

*Chef Jason Crispin, Gourmand Cooking School, Point Pleasant Beach*

Yields 4-8 individual soufflés*

3 Tbsp. unsalted butter, plus extra for greasing the dish
1/4 cup finely grated Parmesan
3 Tbsp. all-purpose flour
1 cup cold milk
2 Tbsp. combined chopped fresh herbs
(savory, rosemary, thyme, sage, oregano, chives)
1/2 tsp. kosher salt and
1/4 tsp. ground black pepper
2 oz. finely chopped bacon
Pinch cayenne pepper
Pinch nutmeg
4 extra-large egg yolks, at room temperature
4 oz. blue cheese, chopped
5 extra-large egg whites, room temperature
1/8 tsp. cream of tartar

Preheat the oven to 400 degrees F. Butter the inside of the soufflé dishes with "extra" butter and sprinkle soufflé dishes evenly with breadcrumbs or parmesan cheese.

In a small saucepan over medium heat melt the butter with the bacon and cook for 2-3 minutes.

When bacon has released its fat into the butter and has begun to crisp add the salt, black pepper, cayenne pepper, nutmeg and fresh herbs and cook for an additional 1-2 minutes.

Using a whisk or wooden spoon, stir in the flour (forming a roux), stirring constantly, for 2 minutes. Whisk in the milk and cook the mixture over medium heat, whisking constantly, for 1-2 minutes, until mixture is thick and smooth. Off the heat, while still hot, whisk in the Romano and Blue cheeses. Add the egg yolks, one at a time until well combined, making sure the yolks are not allowed to scramble. Transfer to a large mixing bowl.

In a separate mixing bowl, combine the egg whites, cream of tartar and a pinch of salt and beat with an electric mixer with whip attachment on high speed until the mixture becomes glossy and stiff peaks are formed. Set aside.

Whisk 1/4 of the egg whites into the cheese and milk "base" to lighten the mixture. FOLD in the remaining egg whites in 2 batches making sure to keep the mixture light and fluffy.

Pour into the soufflé dishes, and then smooth the top (without pressing or flattening the mixture down). Draw a large circle on top with the spatula or the back of a small knife to help the soufflé rise evenly. Place the soufflés on a sheet pan or cookie tray in the middle of the oven. Turn the temperature down to 375 degrees F and bake for 10-12 minutes (don't peek) until the soufflés have puffed up and become golden brown. Serve Immediately

*\* Recipe generally can make 4-8 individual soufflés depending on ramekin size...
Larger ramekins will yield less. This recipe can also be used to prepare 1 "family style" soufflé in an 8 cup soufflé dish. Cook the "family style" soufflé at the same temperature but increase the cooking time to 25-30 minutes*

**Chef Jason Crispin** owns and operates the Gourmand Cooking School in Point Pleasant Beach, NJ. The school features group classes throughout the year and also does private events.

*(Photo on left courtesy Betsy Belt and John Carothers)*

# Spinach & Pancetta Strata

*Boardwalk Breakfast Empire, Food Network,*
*The Great Food Truck Race, representing Sea Bright, NJ*

Preheat oven to 350 degrees F. In a small saucepan over medium heat melt the butter with the bacon and cook for 2-3 minutes.

When bacon has released its fat into the butter and has begun to crisp add the salt, black pepper, cayenne pepper, nutmeg and fresh herbs and cook for an additional 1-2 minutes.

Heat oil in heavy skillet over medium heat, add pancetta and saute pancetta until crisp and golden about 5 minutes, remove pancetta to a bowl. Add onions to pan drippings in the same skillet and saute until translucent, about 4 minutes. Add spinach and garlic. Saute over medium heat until garlic is tender, stir in 1/2 tsp. of salt and 1/4 tsp. of pepper nutmeg add the pancetta.

Place half of cubed bread in a buttered 3-quart (13" X 9") baking dish. Sprinkle 1/2 the cheese over the bread, then top with 1/2 of the spinach mixture. Repeat layering.

Whisk the milk, eggs, remaining 1/2 tsp. salt and 1/4 tsp. of pepper in a large bowl and pour evenly over the strata. Chill the strata, covered with plastic wrap at least 2 hours and up to 12 hours.

Bake strata uncovered until puffed and golden brown, and cooked through, 40 minutes. Let stand 5 minutes before serving. Enjoy!

Serves 6 – 8

2 Tbsp. olive oil
4 oz. thinly sliced pancetta, coarsely chopped
1 small onion, chopped
1 (10 oz.) box chopped frozen spinach thawed and drained
2 garlic cloves minced
1 tsp. salt
1/2 tsp. fresh ground pepper
1/2 tsp. grated nutmeg
8 cups cubed Italian bread
1/2 cup grated Parmesan
3 cups whole milk
10 extra-large eggs

**Joanne Garelli** was invited by the Food Network to captain a food truck on The Great Food Truck Race Season 4 after the restaurant she and her husband Steve operated for 37 years, Steve's Breakfast and Lunch in Sea Bright, NJ, was destroyed by Superstorm Sandy. She was joined in the race by friends Ilene Winters and Timothy Boulous.

**Joanne Garelli (far right) with NJ Governor Chris Christie and Boardwalk Breakfast Empire teammates Ilene Winters and Timothy Boulous.**

*Savoring the Shore*

# Eggs with Creamy Bacon Grits

*Kate Morgan Jackson, Framed Cooks, www.framedcooks.com*

1 cup grits
2 Tbsp. butter
Salt and pepper
4 eggs, soft cooked your favorite way
(poached, fried or soft-boiled)
6 slices bacon, cooked and crumbled

Prepare grits according to package directions. Grits usually take about 45 minutes to their best consistency. Stir in butter until fully melted. Taste and season with salt and fresh ground pepper as needed. Reserve a little of the crumbled bacon and stir the rest into the grits until evenly distributed.

Divide the grits between bowls. Nestle the cooked eggs into the grits and sprinkle with reserved bacon. Just before serving, break into each egg so the yolk melts down into the grits, and grind a little more fresh pepper on top. Enjoy at once!

**Kate Morgan Jackson** is a food writer for The Morris County Daily Record which you can find online at *www.northjersey.com/food_dining*. Her food blog is *www.framedcooks.com* where she notes, "I really do love to cook, and I really do cook every day...but the catch is, it has to be ready in 30 minutes or less, from walk in the kitchen to sitting on the table ready to be eaten. (Except for weekends when I am perfectly happy to spend all day in the kitchen.)"

# Celebration Breakfast Casserole

*Cheryl Larkin*

Serves 8 – 10

6 cups approximately hashed brown style potatoes (defrosted if frozen)*
6 tsp. dried minced onion (do not use with Southwest potatoes)
3 cups shredded sharp cheddar cheese
2 packages frozen sausage links
1 dozen eggs
1/2-1 cup heavy cream
Salt and pepper
Optional 1/4 cup minced fresh parsley

Preheat oven to 350 degrees F. Spray 9" X 13" casserole with non-stick spray. Add potatoes. Sprinkle with minced onion and salt and pepper (skip this step if using Southwest style potatoes.) Top with shredded cheese. Arrange a row of sausage links down center of dish lengthwise and then create "pockets" for one dozen eggs by arranging additional sausages between center row and edge of dish. Crack one egg into each pocket. Pour a bit of cream on each egg yolk and sprinkle with salt and pepper. Bake for 30 -45 minutes at 350 degrees F or until eggs turn white and yolks are set. Sprinkle with fresh parsley if desired before serving.

*We use Simply Potatoes from the refrigerator section. We sometimes use just their regular hashed browns, sometimes use the Southwest hashed browns, and sometimes mix the two.*

# Jersey Style Breakfast Sandwich

*Kate Kurelja*

1 serving

Hard roll (with poppy seeds!)
1 egg
2 thin slices of Taylor Ham or pork roll
2 slices of American cheese
Salt
Pepper
Ketchup

*A classic favorite in the Garden State*

Heat an iron skillet over moderately high heat. When hot, add the Taylor Ham slices. Let cook for about 2 minutes until the edges begin to crisp and fat begins to render. Flip both pieces of ham, then break the egg and add to the skillet. As the white firms, flip the egg and gently press the center with the back of a spatula to break the yolk. Place one slice of cheese on the egg, the other slice on one piece of Taylor Ham. While those heat through slice the hard roll in half. Place one slice Taylor Ham on the bottom half of the roll, top with the cheese covered Taylor Ham and finally the egg and cheese. Liberally sprinkle with salt, pepper and a dollop of ketchup (or as we say – SPK).

# Baked Blueberry-Stuffed French Toast

*Linda Chell Rooney*

(Recipe can be doubled, using a rectangular baking dish.)

Cut baguette into 3/4" slices. Arrange a single layer in a buttered square baking dish. Arrange cream cheese cubes, one on each slice of bread. Sprinkle blueberries evenly over bread. Top with another layer of bread slices and press down lightly. Pour egg mixture over all. Cover with foil and refrigerate overnight.

Preheat oven to 350 degrees F. Place foil-covered baking dish in lower third of oven, bake for 30 minutes. Remove foil and bake for additional 30 minutes. Serve with warmed maple syrup or blueberry syrup.

Serves 4

French baguette
8 oz. cream cheese, cut into cubes
1 cups fresh blueberries

Whisk together:

6 eggs
2 cups milk
1 tsp. vanilla extract
1 Tbsp. cinnamon

# Sour Cream Coffee Cake

*Mueller's Bakery, Bay Head, NJ*

Cream butter and sugar 3-4 min. until light. Add eggs one at a time scraping bowl after each. Add vanilla and sour cream. Sift all dry ingredients and add to above. Finish mixing at end with spatula. Put half batter in greased 13 x 9 pan.Sprinkle half cinnamon nut mixture on top of batter. Top with remaining batter and sprinkle rest of cinnamon mix on top. Bake at 350 degrees F for about 40-45 minutes until toothpick comes out clean.

1-1/2 sticks butter
1-1/2 cups sugar
3 eggs
2 tsp. vanilla
10 oz. sour cream
2 cups cake flour
1/2 cup all-purpose flour
2 tsp. baking powder
1/2 tsp. baking soda
1/2 tsp. sea salt

**Cinnamon nut mixture:**

Put all ingredients in food processor and mix until ground up.

1/4 cup white sugar
1/2 cup brown sugar
2 tsp. cinnamon
1/2 cup pecans

*Savoring the Shore*

# Pat's Irish Soda Bread

*Pat Kurelja*

5 cups all-purpose flour
1/4 lb. butter
5 Tbsp. sugar
2 cups raisins
1-1/4 tsp. baking soda
2 cups buttermilk
2-1/2 tsp. baking powder
2 eggs
1-1/4 tsp. salt
1 Tbsp. caraway seed

In a large bowl, combine first 5 ingredients. Work butter into flour then add raisins and caraway seed.

In another bowl beat eggs and add to buttermilk. Combine wet and dry ingredients. Make a well in the flour and pour wet ingredients into the center and work to combine. Add flour as needed.

Spray the bottom of 2 glass pie plates. Divide the dough into equal parts and place in pie plates.

Cut a cross in the dough and bake at 350 degrees F for 50 minutes.

Let cool 10 minutes in the plates and then remove to a wire rack. Cover with a towel while cooling.

*Hints:* I use 1 cup each of golden and regular raisins. Caraway seeds are optional. Texture is key – too much flour will make it crumbly. Too little four will make it cakey. Enjoy every attempt to get it just right for you.

Pat and family's shore town is Beach Haven, NJ.

# Buttermilk Biscuits with Strawberry Butter

*Chef Karyn Jarmer, My Kitchen Witch, Monmouth Beach, NJ*

1 cup of vegetable shortening plus a bit more to grease the pan
4-1/2 tsp. dry yeast
2 Tbsp. of sugar plus a pinch that you will add to the warm water and yeast
2 Tbsp. warm water
5 cups of all-purpose flour
1 tsp. of baking soda
2 Tbsp. of baking powder
1 tsp. salt
2 cups low fat buttermilk

Preheat oven to 350 degrees F. Get your yeast rising by dissolving yeast in warm water and add that pinch of sugar. Grease pan with a bit of shortening. In mixer, add all dry ingredients at slow speed. Add shortening, buttermilk and yeast and continue to blend until dough starts to stick to paddle. Place dough on board with dusted flour. Spread gently to about 1 inch thick and using a 2 inch biscuit cutter start twisting away, placing all cut biscuits on greased pan. Bake for up to 20 minutes or until golden brown.

## Strawberry Butter

Blend one cup of softened salted butter with 6 Tbsp. of strawberry preserves.

# Betty Height's Island Beach Jam

Pick ripe beach plums, remove chaff, wash and pit. Put pitted plums in an enamel pot and cook for about 20 to 30 minutes. DO NOT ADD WATER. When plums are done put through a food mill to make puree.

To make jam, wash 12 to 14 eight-ounce jars in soapy water, rinse and boil jars for 10 minutes. Remove and prepare lids and screw tops.

In a large enamel pot measure two over-full quarts of pureed beach plums, five pounds of sugar and one box of powered Sure Jell. Follow the directions on the Sure Jell box. Pour jam into the jars, put on the lids and tighten with the screw tops. Sterilize sealed jars by placing them in a large pot, cover with water, and boil for 10 minutes. Remove jars and store in a cool, dry place.

Two over-full quarts of pureed beach plums
One 5-pound bag of sugar
One box of Sure Jell (powdered)

*"This recipe is from the Friends of Island Beach State Park's "Island Beach Plums" recipe book and was contributed by Betty Height, of Point Pleasant. She and her husband, Howard, have one of the "shacks" that still exist in the park, and have been picking beach plums at Island Beach to make jelly, jam and muffins for years. They are also members of the nonprofit, all-volunteer Friends group which was formed in 1996 to enhance interpretive, educational, recreational and research programs, and events at Island Beach State Park in Seaside Park, NJ. Our biggest fundraiser of the year is the annual Beach Plum Festival, held in September.*

*The wild fruit, Prunus Maritima, is native to the sandy North American coast from Maine to Virginia. The fruit is acidic and has a tart, tangy taste that makes delicious jams, jellies, pies, muffins and ice cream. For more information about the Friends, visit http://thefriendsofislandbeach.org." – Bonnie Delaney, volunteer publicity chairperson for Friends of Island Beach State Park*

*(Photo courtesy of Friends of Island Beach State Park)*

*Savoring the Shore*

# Herbes de Provence Rustic No Knead Bread

*John Lee, Black Tie and Flip Flops, Devil Gourmet*

3 cups all-purpose flour
1/4 tsp. active dry yeast
1-3/4 tsp. salt
1 Tbsp. Herbes de Provence
1-1/2 cups plus 2 Tbsp. water
Cornmeal as needed

*"This bread is almost effortless to make because it requires no kneading. Instead, the dough is allowed to slowly rise over a long period of time. Then it is baked in a preheated covered cast-iron pot, which helps produce a crispy, bakery-style crust on the finished loaf." – John Lee*

In a large bowl, combine the flour, yeast, salt, Herbes de Provence. Add 1-5/8 cups water and stir until blended; the dough will be shaggy and very sticky. Cover the bowl with plastic wrap. Let the dough rest at warm room temperature (about 70 degrees F) until the surface is dotted with bubbles, 12 to 18 hours.

Place the dough on a lightly floured work surface. Sprinkle the dough with a little flour and fold the dough over onto itself once or twice. Cover loosely with plastic wrap and let rest for 15 minutes.

Using just enough flour to keep the dough from sticking to the work surface or your fingers, gently and quickly shape the dough into a ball. Generously coat a cotton towel, preferably a flour sack towel (not terry cloth), with cornmeal. Put the dough, seam side down, on the towel and dust with more flour or cornmeal. Cover with another cotton towel and let rise until the dough is more than double in size and does not readily spring back when poked with a finger, about 2 hours.

(Photo courtesy of John Lee)

At least 30 minutes before the dough is ready, put a 2-3/4-quart cast-iron pot in the oven and preheat the oven to 450 degrees F.

Carefully remove the pot from the oven. Slide your hand under the towel and turn the dough over, seam side up, into the pot; it may look like a mess, but that is OK. Shake the pan once or twice if the dough is unevenly distributed; it will straighten out as it bakes. Cover with the lid and bake for 30 minutes. Uncover and continue baking until the loaf is browned, 15 to 30 minutes more.

Transfer the pot to a wire rack and let cool for 10 minutes. Using oven mitts turn the pot on its side and gently turn the bread; it will release easily. Makes one 1-1/2 lb. loaf.

*"This is the bread I made for the Breads and Spreads Class at Williams Sonoma Montclair in October 2010. That bread was based on a recipe for a Walnut Rustic Bread attributed to the "Cooking In Cast Iron" book. A little googling and I found very similar recipes that were adapted from Sullivan Street Bakery (NYC) and Mark Bittman, "The Secret of Great Bread: Let Time Do the Work," The New York Times, Nov. 8, 2006." – John Lee*

# Little Bites and Pours

# Ahi Tuna on a Crispy Wonton Chip

*Chef Mike Jurusz*

Serves 4

1/2 lb. of Sashimi tuna
12 pieces fried wonton skins
to make chips
1/2 cup pickled ginger (Gari)
1/4 cup wasabi
(Japanese green horseradish)
1/2 cup kabayaki sauce
1/2 cup tempura crumbs
1 bunch diced scallion

Place the ginger and wasabi on the bottom of the wonton chip. Place a slice of tuna on top. Add the kabayaki sauce, crumbs and scallion.

**Chef Mike Jurusz** has been named to Best Chefs America 2013. He is the owner/chef at Chef Mike's ABG (Atlantic Bar and Grill) in South Seaside Park, NJ.

# Fresh Shucked Oysters on the 1/2 Shell with Spicy Bloody Mary Granite

*Chef Mike Jurusz*

Yields two dozen oysters

1/2 bottle of your favorite Bloody
Mary mix
3 Tbsp. horseradish
1 Tbsp. Tabasco
Cracked black pepper to taste
2 lemons
1 cup water
24 fresh shucked oysters (your choice)
1/2 cup of your favorite vodka

In a large bowl mix the Bloody Mary mix, horseradish, Tabasco, cracked black pepper, water, and the juice of the two lemons. Mix well and place in a shallow pan. Wrap with plastic and freeze for a day.

Shuck the oysters and place on shaved ice. Chip away the Bloody Mary ice and place a small chuck on each oyster. Splash some of the vodka on top and serve.

**Chef Mike Jurusz** has been named to Best Chefs America 2013. He is the owner/chef at Chef Mike's ABG (Atlantic Bar and Grill) in South Seaside Park, NJ.

*"The oysters eat algae which naturally exist, in abundance. The oysters remove excess nutrients from the water, improving water quality and increasing dissolved oxygen levels. In the northeast, oysters are meant to be a part of our estuaries. Depletion of wild oysters, as a result of over harvesting, has really hurt our waterways. The more oyster farms we have, the healthier and cleaner our water will be."*

*–Matt Gregg of Forty North Oyster Farm, Mantoloking, NJ, as reported by Deborah Smith, Founder and Executive Editor, Jersey Bites, The Dodge Blog, Oct. 24, 2012*

*(Photo on opposite page courtesy of Matt Gregg, Forty North Oyster Farm)*

*Little Bites and Pours*

# Oysters Mantoloking

*Matt Gregg, Forty North Oyster Farm, Mantoloking, NJ*

Shuck oyster(s), without spilling the briny liquor. Add a small layer of breadcrumbs until the meat of the oyster is no longer visible. Add diced shallot and rosemary. Top with sliced provolone and bake or grill at 350 degrees F for 10-15 minutes or until edges are golden brown. Always purchase oysters from a trusted local source. Ask to see the harvest tags to ensure oysters are fresh and live.

Oysters (one per person
   as an appetizer)
Breadcrumbs
Shallot
Rosemary
Sliced Provolone

# Michael's Shrimp

*Cathy Craven*

Put raw shrimp in bowl. Cover with 3/4 of dressing, reserving the rest for later. Squeeze the juice of four lemons over the bowl. Marinate for 30 minutes. Meanwhile bring grill to 400 degrees F.

Using a slotted spoon transfer marinated shrimp to a mesh cooking basket sprayed with non-stick cooking spray. Cook for two minutes on each side or until shrimp turn pink. Transfer to serving plate. Drizzle with reserved dressing and juice of 4 remaining lemons.

Michael's shrimp has been a family favorite for years, often served on a deck at LBI with Cosmopolitans.

Serves 6 – 8

2 lbs. fresh raw shrimp, cleaned
One package dry Italian dressing mix
   made according to package
   directions with olive oil and
   vinegar
8 lemons cut in quarters

# Clam Dip

*Andrea DeRosa*

Preheat oven to 375 degrees F. Mix all ingredients together except light cream. Put in baking dish, pour light cream on top and bake 25 minutes.

*Hint:* always double this recipe at least! Enjoy!

2 cans doxee chopped clams
   (1 can drained)
1/2 cup melted butter
3/4 cup bread crumbs
3/4 cup crushed Ritz crackers
1 large diced onion
1/2 tsp. paprika
1/2 cup light cream

# Chicken Wings in Garlic Sauce

*Chef Jason Crispin, Gourmand Cooking School, Point Pleasant Beach, NJ*

2 dozen chicken wings
Flour, for dredging
2 Tbsp. paprika
Salt and pepper
1/4 cup Spanish olive oil
Pinch red pepper flakes
1 bay leaf
2 lemons, halved
10 roasted cloves garlic
1/4 cup chopped fresh oregano
1/4 cup Spanish sherry
2 cups low-sodium chicken broth

Rinse the chicken wings in cold water and pat dry with paper towels. Place flour in a shallow platter and season it by adding paprika, salt and pepper. Toss to incorporate then dredge the wings in the flour.

Heat oil in a skillet and brown the chicken wings on all sides. Remove the chicken from the pan and set aside on a platter. Add the pepper flakes, bay leaf, lemons, garlic, oregano, sherry, and chicken broth to the pan. Cook for 2 minutes to evaporate the alcohol. Return the chicken to the pan. Cover the pan and simmer for 15 minutes, or braise in a preheated 375 degree F oven for 20 minutes.

**Chef Jason Crispin** owns and operates the Gourmand Cooking School in Point Pleasant Beach, NJ. The school features group classes throughout the year and also does private events.

# Alice Larkin's Onion Dip

*Debby Larkin*

1 package cream cheese at
room temperature
2 beef bouillon cubes or packets,
dissolved in 2 Tbsp. boiling water
1 Tbsp. Worcestershire sauce
2 - 3 Tbsp. grated onion
(to your taste)

Mix all ingredients together at least a few hours before serving. Serve with potato chips or raw vegetables – carrot and celery sticks, pepper strips, broccoli or cauliflower florets. I mix it all in a food processor starting with the onion which I grate fine, then add the rest and mix it all together. If you don't want to do that, finely grate the onion into a bowl, add the remaining ingredients and mix with a hand mixer.

# Guacamole

*Chef Ivy Stark, Dos Caminos*

*"Dos Caminos' guacamole is probably our most famous dish. It has been voted the best guacamole in many different polls. We prepare it tableside in a lava stone molcajete according to each guest's specifications. The spice level can be raised or lowered by adjusting the amount of chile you add.*

*What makes ours so good? First, guacamole is at its best when made just before serving it. Another key to success is California-grown Haas avocados because they have a creamier, denser texture than all other varieties. We serve the dip with warm, hand-cut tortilla chips. This recipe may be doubled as many times as you like." – Chef Ivy Stark*

In a medium size bowl, use the back of a spoon to mash 1 tablespoon of the cilantro, 1 teaspoon onion, 1 teaspoon of minced chile, and 1/2 teaspoon salt together against the bottom of the bowl.

Add the avocados and gently mash them with a fork until chunky-smooth. Fold the remaining cilantro, onion, and chile into the mixture. Stir in tomatoes and lime juice, taste to adjust the seasonings, and serve with a basket of warm corn tortilla chips.

**Chef Ivy Stark** is Executive Chef of Dos Caminos, New York, and is ranked among New York's top chefs. Dos Caminos is also located at Harrah's Atlantic City Resort.

Makes 4 servings

- 2 Tbsp. finely chopped cilantro leaves
- 2 tsp. finely chopped white onion
- 2 tsp. minced jalapeño or Serrano chilies, seeds and membranes removed, if desired
- 1/2 tsp. kosher salt
- 2 large ripe avocados, preferably California Haas, peeled and seeded
- 2 Tbsp. cored, seeded, and finely chopped plum tomatoes (1 small tomato)
- 2 tsp. freshly squeezed lime juice

# Tony's Mango Guac

*Tony Kennette, Kennette Productions, www.kennetteproductions.com*

Using your favorite fine chopping method, prepare and combine the mango, cilantro, and jalapeno into a pulpy "salsa texture." Slice or scoop out the avocados into a bowl. Then evenly mix the mango pulp into the avocado. Season with salt and pepper to taste.

- 2 ripe avocados
- 1 ripe mango
- Fresh cilantro from grandma's garden (1/2 - 1 Tbsp. chopped)
- 2 of the lime wedges from grandma's Sapphire on the rocks
- 1/2-1 fresh jalapeno (to taste)
- Ground pepper
- Salt

# Hummus

*Sarah Pritchard, PritchardPhotography@Live.com*

Mix all ingredients in a food processor until smooth. Serve with toasted pita bread, bagel chips or even pretzels.

- 16 oz. can chick peas, drained but save the juice
- Juice of 1/2 a fresh lemon
- 2 large cloves garlic
- 1/4 cup Tahini (or substitute 2 Tbsp. olive oil)
- 2 Tbsp. chick pea juice (discard the rest)
- 1 tsp. salt

*Savoring the Shore*

## Santa Fe Salsa
*Suzanne Presti*

1/2 cup fresh corn
1/2 cup black olives, chopped
1/2 cup red pepper, diced
2 cloves garlic, minced
2 ripe avocados, peeled and diced
3 Tbsp. olive oil
1 Tbsp. lemon jjuice
1/3 tsp. red wine vinegar
1 tsp. oregano
1/2 tsp. pepper
Salt to taste

Combine all ingredients except avocados. Add them just before serving. Serve with tortilla chips.

*"This is a crowd pleaser! Whether we pack it and bring it to the beach in the evening or serve it right outside on our deck, it's perfect with good friends and good Margaritas!"*
*– Suzanne Presti*

## Peach Summer Salsa
*Michele Robertson*

2 cups white peaches, pitted and chopped
1 cup chopped and seeded cucumber
1/2 cup red bell pepper
1/2 cup red onion
2 Tbsp. fresh mint, chopped
1 tsp. hot red pepper flakes
2 Tbsp. white balsamic vinegar
Salt and pepper to taste

Combine all ingredients and serve on your favorite tortilla chips.

**Tent houses at Ocean Grove, NJ**
*(Photo courtesy Tony Kennette, www.kennetteproductions.com)*

## Dill Dip
*Rosalie Pembridge*

1 cup of sour cream
1 cup of mayonnaise
1-1/3 Tbsp. dried dill weed
1-1/3 Tbsp. dried onion
A pinch of garlic salt

Combine all ingredients in a bowl and refrigerate overnight to let the flavors meld together. Serve with raw vegetables.

# Meatballs and/or Cocktail Sausages in Sauce
*Debby Larkin*

*"The most important part of this recipe is the sauce. Sometimes I just buy a package of cocktail franks or sausages and put them in the sauce. If you want to get fancy, make the meatballs." – Debby Larkin*

### Sauce for Cocktail Meatballs and/or Franks

Combine all ingredients. Heat to boiling. Simmer gently for 10 minutes with meatballs or cocktail franks. Serve in a chafing dish with tooth picks.

2 cups sweet Italian vermouth
1/4 cup fresh lemon juice
1/4 cup soy sauce
1 can undiluted tomato soup
Few drops Tabasco sauce (to taste)

### Alice Larkin's Swedish Meatballs

Mix together all ingredients. Shape into bite sized meatballs. Spray a sheet pan with Pam and put meatballs on it. Bake at 350 degrees F for 45 minutes.

1 lb. ground beef
2 slices of toast, cut in pieces.
    Wet with water and wring out.
1 medium onion, chopped.
    Cook to soften.
1 egg
Salt, pepper and chopped parsley,
    to taste

# Hot Cheese Appetizer
*Debby Larkin*

Preheat oven to 350 degrees F.

This is very easy to make in a food processor. I just chunk up the cheese and put it with the onion and mayo all together in the bowl and whiz them together with the steel blade. If you don't have a food processor, then grate the cheese, chop the onion, and mix it all in a bowl till all is combined.

8 oz. cheddar cheese, grated
2 - 3 Tbsp. finely grated or chopped onion
2 Tbsp. mayonnaise

Then take the cheese mixture, put it in an oven proof dish and bake at 350 for about 20 minutes. You may need to stir it after about 10 minutes to get it to melt evenly. Serve with crackers. Be careful because you will burn the roof of your mouth if you dig in too soon after it's out of the oven.

This recipe can be doubled, and the quantities are not absolutely exact. It's great to throw together at a shore house with not much equipment and you get a great dish for cocktail hour.

*"For every one of our 34 years together, my husband, Joe Kramer, and I spent part of our summer on Long Beach Island. We spent many happy times with family and friends, and always enjoyed the Golden Hour on the deck with drinks and hors d'oeuvres. The hot cheese was a huge favorite of the whole family's, and was absolutely mandatory. They would have eaten it every night! Dinners were always full of fresh NJ produce. You can't beat a Jersey beefsteak tomato or corn on the cob. Cassidy's Fish Market has the freshest fish, and Michael Craven could always grill up some really fine dinners. Gaby Jordan makes the best salads in the world. I always made tacos at least once because there were so many different fillings that satisfied meat lovers and vegetarians alike. Gisela Jordan made fabulous dishes, all exquisitely presented and healthy as well as delicious! Desserts were simple. The jingle of the ice cream truck or a quick run to the Dairy Queen. It was heaven." – Debby Larkin*

*Savoring the Shore*

# Hot Corned Beef Dip

*Betsy Belt*

1/2 lb. corned beef, chopped fine
1 cup mayonnaise
1 cup Swiss cheese, grated
1 cup sauerkraut, drained and chopped
2 Tbsp. horseradish
2 cloves garlic, chopped fine

Mix all ingredients. Heat at 350 degrees F for 30 minutes. Serve with garlic bagel chips.

# Blueberry Iced Tea

*Ren Miller, Editor in Chief, DesignNJ Magazine*

1 cup of fresh blueberries
3 cups of brewed green tea
Ice

Puree the blueberries and 1 cup of the tea in a blender until smooth. Strain into a pitcher and add the remaining tea and ice cubes.

*"My wife and I first tasted blueberry tea at a friend's home many years ago when we lived in Chester County, Pennsylvania. It's a healthy, delicious drink to enjoy on a hot summer day."*

# Watermelon Agua Fresca

*Chef Ivy Stark, Dos Caminos*

16 cups cubed seedless red watermelon
2 cups water
2/3 cup sugar
1 bunch fresh mint
1/2 cup fresh lime juice
Club soda
Lime slices, for garnish

Combine the watermelon, water, sugar and mint in a blender; puree. Pour through a coarse strainer into a large container. Stir in lime juice. Refrigerate until well chilled, about 4 hours. To serve, fill highball glass with ice, fill glass 2/3 full with watermelon mixture, top with club soda and garnish with lime.

**Chef Ivy Stark** is Executive Chef of Dos Caminos, New York, and is ranked among New York's top chefs. Dos Caminos is also located at Harrah's Atlantic City Resort.

# Chocolate Martini

*Debbie Rutherford*

Vanilla vodka
Creme de cacao
Godiva chocolate liqueur

In shaker with ice, combine:

1 part vanilla vodka

2 parts creme de cacao

1 part chocolate liqueur

Shake and pour into glass drizzled with chocolate syrup.

# Brenne Gentle Fizz (anything but gentle)

*Allison Patel, mixologist Warren Bobrow*

Wash the glasses out with the Barr Hill Vodka (pour into your mouth as not to waste even a precious drop!). Add all the ingredients except the Perrier to a Boston Shaker filled with ice. Hard shake and double strain into coupes, finish with a splash or two of the Perrier Sparkling Water. Add a final dash of the lemon bitters and garnish with a sprig of lemon thyme.

*This recipe was originally published at http://blog.drinkupny.com/2013/07/brenne-gentle-fizz.html. Reprinted with permission.*

**Allison Patel** is president of Local Infusions, LLC, developers of Brenne Whisky. Her family's home in Ocean City, NJ was destroyed by Hurricane Sandy. She has submitted three recipes to Savoring the Shore to support Sandy rebuilding efforts in NJ.

Serves two

3 oz. Brenne French Single Malt Whisky

1 oz. (for the wash) Caledonia Spirits "Barr Hill" Vodka (made from Raw Honey)

1/4 oz. freshly squeezed lime juice

1/4 oz. freshly squeezed lemon juice

1 oz. raw honey simple syrup (one part honey, one part water, bring to boil on stove then cool before using)

Fresh lemon thyme leaf (no wood, please) crushed to release its perfume

A few dashes of The Bitter Truth Lemon Bitters

3 oz. Perrier Sparkling Natural Mineral Water in Lime essence

# Best Ever Cosmopolitans

*Debby Larkin*

Put all ingredients in a shaker or pitcher and mix well. Shake or stir your preference. Strain into a cocktail glass. A slice of fresh lime garnish is optional.

*\* Can substitute any orange liqueur such as Cointreau or Grand Marnier*

For one drink:

1/2 oz. Rose's Lime Juice
1 oz. Triple Sec*
1-1/2 oz. vodka
Splash of cranberry juice to make it pink!

For two drinks:

1 oz. Rose's Lime Juice
2 oz. Triple Sec*
3 oz. vodka
Splash of cranberry juice to make it pink!

# Brooklyn Blossom*

*Noon Summer (Titled Boston's Best Mixologist, from restaurant Moksa)*

*\*"A fun play on the Manhattan using Sorel instead of sweet vermouth. Also a dedication to Allison Patel using Brenne, her rockin' French Single Malt!" – Noon Summer*

2.5 oz. Brenne French Single Malt

1.5 oz. Sorel (distillery in Red Hook was destroyed by Sandy and has since rebuilt)

1 oz. Dolin Dry

1 Dash Angustura

Garnish with twist and hibiscus blossom

*Savoring the Shore*

# Étienne Pellot "Montvieux" Cocktail
# for two soon to be quite drenched sailors

*Allison Patel, mixologist Warren Bobrow*

Serves two

3 oz. Brenne Whisky from France
1/2 oz. Tenneyson Absinthe
(for the wash)
2 oz. Royal Rose Simple Syrup of
Cardamom and Clove
2 oz. freshly squeezed
pink grapefruit juice
2 oz. (in each glass) Perrier Sparkling
Natural Mineral Water
(Pink Grapefruit)
2 dashes in each glass
Peychaud's Bitters

First cool the glasses with ice, water and the Tenneyson Absinthe, set aside to cool (essential). Cut a grapefruit zest in the style of a Crusta (1 long thread).

To a Boston Shaker filled 3/4 with ice add Brenne Whisky, Royal Rose Simple Syrup and fresh grapefruit juice. Close and shake for 15 seconds to chill it down.

Pour out the Tenneyson Absinthe, ice and water from the glasses (preferably into your mouth as not to waste even a drop of this precious liquor). Add one large cube of hand cut ice to the pre-chilled rocks glasses and pour in the shaken cocktail. Add a splash or two of the Pink Grapefruit Perrier Sparkling Natural Mineral Water. Garnish with the grapefruit zest and two shakes of Peychaud's Bitters

*This recipe was originally published at **http://blog.drinkupny.com/2013/07/brenne-gentle-fizz.html**. Reprinted with permission.*

**Allison Patel** is president of Local Infusions, LLC, developers of Brenne Whisky. Her family's home in Ocean City, NJ was destroyed by Hurricane Sandy. She has submitted three recipes to Savoring the Shore to support Sandy rebuilding efforts in NJ.

# Margarita Mix

*Cheryl Larkin*

100 ml Triple Sec orange liqueur
(or to taste)
200 ml Tequila (or to taste)
1 large can frozen Limeade
concentrate, defrosted
One clean, empty 1.75 liter bottle
One fresh lime
1/4 cup kosher salt (to rim glass)

Add first 3 ingredients to 1.75 liter bottle. Fill the rest of the bottle with water allowing room to shake contents. Shake and keep cold. To rim glass, put kosher salt on plate. Rub rim of glass with fresh lime and dip in salt.

# White Sangria

*Chef Marilyn Schlossbach, Langosta Lounge, Asbury Park, NJ*

Combine the wine, juice, and all the fruit pieces in a large pitcher.
Mix well, cover and refrigerate overnight. Enjoy!!!!!

**Chef Marilyn Schlossbach** has been named one of the Best Chefs America 2013. She owns a number of restaurants at the NJ Shore including Langosta Lounge, Asbury Park, NJ.

Makes 18 glasses, 15 minutes preparation

8 cups (64 fl. oz.) dry white wine
2 cups of dry rose
1 cups (64 fl. oz.) pear juice or another white juice
1 cup of passion fruit juice
2 Tbsp. agave nectar
1 cup pear liquor
1/2 medium orange, sliced thin crosswise
1 small pear, diced
1 medium mango, diced
1 pineapple cubed
1 cup of raspberries sliced

# Peach Prosecco Sangria

*Dorothy Friedman*

*"This is a fan favorite at all my summer pool parties. Even those who swear they only drink red wine adore it!" –Dorothy Friedman*

This is for 1 pitcher, but can be doubled for a larger crowd.

1 nectarine, 1 peach and 3 apricots cut in eights.

Soak for 1 hour in 5 oz. peach brandy.

Then, add one 750 bottle chilled Prosecco wine, 1 cup peach nectar (can get in the juice aisle) and add a couple Tbsp. superfine sugar (optional) to taste.

Serve over ice.

Yum!

*Savoring the Shore*

# Forever Unloved Sandy

*Gene Muller, Flying Fish Brewing Company, Somerdale, NJ*

*After Superstorm Sandy struck the state, Flying Fish Brewing Co. joined the many other folks who wanted to help out. They decided to do it by doing what they do best--brew beer. Forever Unloved (F.U.) Sandy was their response as a way to raise funds. The original batch was limited to 80 kegs and generated $45,000 for relief efforts. Based on the overwhelming response, Flying Fish re-released the beer in 750ml bottles to continue its fundraising efforts.*

*Sandy is brewed with a 50/50 blend of Two Row Pale Malt and American White Wheat. It was hopped with experimental hop ADHA 483, donated by the American Dwarf Hop Association, which had never been used in a beer before this one. The beer has a beautiful, tropical nose of mangoes and guavas that accentuates its soft mouthfeel from the wheat and contributes to a truly one-of-a-kind ale – much like the Jersey shore.*

*FU Sandy pairs well with anything you can put on the grill!*

Soups and Sandwiches

# Blender Gazpacho

*Sarah Pritchard, PritchardPhotography@Live.com*

3 large ripe, peeled tomatoes
1 medium onion peeled and quartered
3 cloves garlic
1 tsp. cumin
Water to suit your liking
1 small red pepper
1 tsp. salt
3 Tbsp. wine vinegar
1 tsp. olive oil
Sour cream for garnish

Blend everything except sour cream in blender adding *in order*. After everything is added, blend at high speed, no longer than 4 – 5 seconds. Add a dollop of sour cream when serving.

# BBQ Chicken Chili

*Sue Sinclair Richter*

2 lbs. chicken
2 bottles BBQ sauce

**Part 1:**

Put chicken and BBQ sauce into crock pot. Cook for 4 hours.

1 cup red pepper, diced
1 cup green pepper, diced
3/4 cup onion, diced
2 cups carrots, diced
3/4 cup celery, chopped
2 cans red kidney beans
2 tsp. garlic, chopped
4 cups chicken stock
6 cups (60 oz.) tomato sauce
6 cups diced tomatoes
4 tsp. Worcestershire sauce
1 tsp. crushed red pepper
1/2 cup dried parsley
4 tsp. chili powder
1 tsp. cumin
1 tsp. black pepper

**Part 2:**

Put all "part 2" ingredients into stock pot. Bring to a boil, then simmer until vegetable are tender & chili thickens. Add chicken and BBQ sauce to stockpot. Let simmer.

**Aerial beach view**
*(Photo courtesy Robert Alberding, RCAP/Remote Control Aerial Photography, https//www.facebook.com/RemoteControlAerialPhotography?trf=br_tf)*

# Garden State Gazpacho

*Chef Jason Crispin, Gourmand Cooking School, Point Pleasant Beach, NJ*

Bring 4 quarts of water to a boil. Core the tomatoes and score an X on the bottom of the tomatoes. Plunge the tomatoes into the boiling water and cook for 30 seconds. Remove the tomatoes from the boiling water and place them in an ice bath to stop the cooking process. Remove the skin from the tomatoes and coarsely chop the tomatoes.

In a bowl combine the tomatoes, bell peppers, sundried tomatoes, cucumbers, bread crumbs, Worcestershire sauce, olive oil, vinegar, salt and pepper. In a food processor or blender process half of the mixture until nearly smooth. Process the remaining mixture and vegetable juice and continue to process until the mixture is smooth and well combined.

Chill the soup for several hours or overnight if possible. Just prior to serving, check for seasoning and add additional salt and pepper to taste. Garnish the soup with a mixture of small diced cucumber, red onion, tomato and chopped parsley or cubed bread.

**Chef Jason Crispin** owns and operates the Gourmand Cooking School in Point Pleasant Beach, NJ. The school features group classes throughout the year and also does private events.

Yields 2 quarts

2 cups vegetable juice (V8)
2 lb. vine ripened tomatoes
1 seedless cucumber, peeled and course chopped
2 red bell peppers, seeded and course chopped
4 Tbsp. sundried tomatoes, thin julienne (reconstituted)
2 Tbsp. rice wine vinegar (white wine or champagne vinegar as substitute)
4 Tbsp. extra virgin olive oil
1 tsp. kosher salt
1/2 tsp. black pepper
1/2 tsp. Worcestershire sauce
2 cups fresh bread crumbs (approx. 4 slices white bread)

# Tomato Goat Cheese Jalapeno Soup

*Chef Jacqueline Baldassari, Hell's Kitchen Season 11*

Saute onions, celery, garlic, jalapeno until lightly browned. Add tomatoes, stock, goat cheese.

Stir and cook for one hour on a low medium heat. Take off stove and let cool for 15-20 minutes.

Puree with stick blender. Check salt.

1 large onion rough chopped
1 stalk celery rough chopped
6 jalapeno peppers no seeds, rough chopped
15 pieces of garlic
1 #10 can whole peeled tomatoes
1 log of goat cheese cut up (2.2 lb.)
1 quart unseasoned (no salt) stock

*(Photo opposite page courtesy Gourmand Cooking School)*

*Savoring the Shore*

# My Kitchen Witch Conjures Food Magic
# Fit for a Former President, a Pope and Many Stars

Thanks to the crew of The Rosie O'Donnell show a few years back, New Jersey native and restaurateur **Karyn Jarmer** became known as the **Kitchen Witch**. She had already been working her magic for a few years as a caterer delivering delicious, wholesome food to such television shows as Live with Regis and Kathie Lee, Maury Povitch, Ricki Lake, All My Children, and One Life to Live. The Kitchen Witch nickname came after she pulled a breakfast out of her hat at a moment's notice for Rosie O'Donnell's guest Madonna who has some particular dietary preferences like vegan and unsweetened and was originally scheduled to have lunch.

**Chef Jarmer (aka My Kitchen Witch)** has been involved in the restaurant world since she was a teenager when she started working in the summer at Schneider's Restaurant in Avon, NJ, making ice cream sundaes. When fall and winter came she worked inside as a waitress and a hostess and knew right away that being around food was where she belonged.

After high school graduation she headed to Manhattan where she first worked at Fulton Street Fish Market then started Dock Foodies at Pier 17 at the age of 19. After cooking and bartending around the city for a bit, she started her first catering business in 1993. Her first break into the entertainment world was catering for the Sally Jessy Raphael Show.

Fast forward a few years and Chef Jarmer could no longer resist the call of her home, the New Jersey shore (she grew up in Bradley Beach and Shark River Hills). Here, she loves the quality of life, being able to surf, kayak, paddle board or run the boards in the morning, then cook her heart out. To coin a phrase from one of her favorite movies, "There's no place like home." And so her restaurant, My Kitchen Witch in Monmouth Beach was born.

(Photo courtesy of JoAnne Lense)

Here in the Café she serves "healthy home cooked meals that will soothe your soul." These include breakfast and lunch daily as well as to go items from the attached Magical Market and juices from the Magical Potion Juice Bar. On Friday nights there are BYOB candlelight dinners in the Café, and seating is reserved. She also caters a variety of events.

Five years ago happily "restauranting" and catering events in New Jersey, Chef Jarmer received an offer she couldn't refuse.

"A phone call came asking me to cater a big [entertainment type] event at JFK Airport," she says. At first she declined because "these types of events are always 24/7" feeding everybody from the crew who build the sets to the talent who arrive at show time. "So they asked me to review the paperwork which included the Clintons and the Pope." She said yes and was there with delicious, healthy food during set-construction at the old Pan Am hanger at JFK and when the Pope and other dignitaries arrived.

Since then Chef Jarmer's two worlds have merged and in addition to My Kitchen Witch at the New Jersey shore she also once again caters to the entertainment world. She has four trucks and eight mothers from the shore who help to implement the effort. They've catered shows like Worst Cooks, Project Runway and Project Runway All Stars, and four years of Celebrity Apprentice. A perk of course is seeing celebrities in action, like Cyndi Lauper giving a live concert at the last episode of Celebrity Apprentice during the season that she was on the show. Speaking of concerts, they've also catered Carnegie Hall with Elton John, and were even listed in the Playbill.

At this writing, My Kitchen Witch is catering the feature film "Hits" starring Michael Cera and directed by David Cross and also catering for Nike for the US Open. "In 2012 when we catered for Nike they brought in all these huge mannequins and we wondered what was going on. It ended up being the unveiling of the new NFL uniforms," she says, pointing out that it's fun for her and her team to go into New York for 6 to 8 hours a day and be part of these events, then come back home to sand and sea.

The menu selection is usually up to Chef Jarmer. "I start with the question 'Who am I feeding?'" If it's the crew building the set the menu leans toward comfort foods like macaroni and cheese or meatloaf. When the talent or dignitaries arrive, the fare gets lighter. Either way, there's no doubt that Chef Karyn Jarmer works magic. As she puts it, "It's amazing how you can turn the energy of a shoot around with good food."

*Savoring the Shore*

# Chicken and Stars

*Chef Karyn Jarmer, My Kitchen Witch, Monmouth Beach, NJ*

1 bag fresh carrots
1 head of celery
2 white onions
5 boneless breasts of chicken
12 cups chicken stock
1 cup parmesan cheese
1 cup stars
1 can of whole tomatoes
Parsley, salt and pepper

Boil for 30 minutes chicken breast in water. Let cool. Using a food processor, puree all carrots, celery and onion and put in pot with chicken stock. Squeeze all tomatoes by hand and add any remaining juice from can to pot. Add parmesan and a little salt and pepper. Shred the chicken and add to pot. Toss in stars and bring to boil then reduce heat and simmer for 10 minutes add some parsley and serve it up.

*Check out Chef Jarmer's recipe for Buttermilk Biscuits and Strawberry Jam in the Breakfast, Brunch and Bread section.*

# Santa Fe Corn Chowder

*Bette Jacobson*

Serves 8
2 Tbsp. butter
3 Tbsp. flour
1 cup chopped onion
3/4 tsp. ground cumin
1/2 tsp. garlic salt
1/2 tsp. coriander
4 cups milk
1 – 16 oz. package frozen corn with red and green peppers (if unavailable, substitute canned, drained)
1 15 oz. can black beans rinsed and drained
1-1/2 cups sharp cheddar cheese, shredded
2 Tbsp. cilantro, fresh, chopped

Melt butter in saucepan over medium heat. Cook onions in butter til crisp-tender. Mix flour, cumin, garlic salt and coriander in medium bowl, gradually stir in milk.

Pour milk mixture into onions and then stir in corn and beans. Heat to boiling, stirring constantly. Boil and stir one minute. Remove from heat and stir in 1 cup of the cheese until melted. Top each serving with the remaining cheese and cilantro.

Savoring the Shore

# Chicken Soup

*Chef Tom Colicchio, Craft Restaurants Inc.*

Serves 4

1 chicken, quartered, with bones intact (i.e., do not remove breast meat from breastbone, including necks and giblets)
2 carrots, peeled and cut in half
2 celery stalks, washed and cut in half
2 leeks, washed and sliced in half
2 parsnips, peeled and cut in half
1 onion, peeled and cut in half
1 sprig of fresh thyme
Kosher salt, freshly ground black pepper
1-1/2 cups small shell pasta (optional)
Freshly grated Parmigiano-Reggiano (optional)
Coarse sea salt

*"This soup is a typical, relaxed, Sunday evening meal for me and my family. I serve this soup the way my grandmother did, with the Parmigiano and olive oil. Every grandmother has a chicken soup recipe, so mine certainly isn't the definitive recipe, but it's still my favorite, and I enjoy sharing that with my kids today the same way my grandmother did with me."*
*– Chef Tom Colicchio*

Place 1 gallon water and the chicken in a stockpot and bring to a simmer over medium heat. Simmer gently, skimming regularly, until broth is fragrant, for about 30 minutes. Add the vegetables and thyme and continue to simmer for another 20 minutes. Season with salt and pepper.

Bring a large pot of salted water to a boil over high heat. Add the pasta and cook until tender, about 8 minutes. Drain and divide the cooked pasta among 4 bowls.

Remove the chicken with a slotted spoon and place on a serving dish. Ladle the broth and vegetables over the pasta and serve with grated Parmigiano, more freshly ground black pepper, and a drizzle of extra virgin olive oil, if desired. Sprinkle the chicken with coarse sea salt and serve along side the soup.

From **Craft of Cooking,** Clarkson Potter, 2003, reprinted with permission of author.

*"Born in Elizabeth, New Jersey, Colicchio spent his childhood immersed in food, cooking with his mother and grandmother. It was his father, however, who suggested that he make a career of it. Colicchio taught himself to cook with the help of Jacques Pépin's legendary illustrated manuals on French cooking, La Technique and La Méthode. At the age of 17, he made his kitchen debut in his native town of Elizabeth at Evelyn's Seafood Restaurant." –Tom Colicchio **Biography, www.bravotv.com***

# Marilyn's Roasted Turkey Matzo Ball Soup

*Chef Marilyn Schlossbach, Langosta Lounge, Asbury Park, NJ*

## Stock:

One whole turkey for meat and for 5 to 6 lbs. turkey bones to make stock, including necks and feet coarsely chopped; may use store bought chicken stock – no MSG, Knorr's makes a good one (you will need 10-12 cups).

COOK - 1 whole TURKEY, washed and patted dry – rubbed with garlic, 1/4 pound of butter melted, sea salt and pepper and roast in the oven until cooked  (time depends on the size of the bird – roast at 350 degrees F and baste with juices and butter). Carve turkey and use the bones for making stock. Shred the turkey meat and set aside for finished soup.

Place the poultry bones in a 6 or 7-quart pot, pour cold water over to cover, and bring to a rolling boil. Skim off the foam and fat that collects on the top. Add the remaining ingredients, lower the heat to a simmer, and simmer uncovered for 2 to 3 hours, skimming as necessary. Strain through a fine-mesh strainer into a clean bowl and cool. Can be made a few days in advance. Discard the hardened layer of fat before using.

1 medium carrot, peeled, trimmed, and cut into 1-inch slices
1 medium onion, peeled, trimmed, and quartered
1 small celery stalk, trimmed, and cut into 1-inch slices
1 small leek, cleaned, trimmed, and cut into 1-inch slices
1 sprig fresh thyme
1 sprig rosemary
1 sprig sage
3 sprigs fresh parsley with stems
1 bay leaf
1/2 tsp. whole white peppercorns

## Matzo Balls:

Chop seasonings very fine then fry in oil. When clear, add cup of boiling water; then cool a few minutes. Add matzo meal and well beaten egg yolks, then fold in stiffly beaten egg whites. Form into small balls and drop into boiling chicken soup or you can drop them into boiling salted water. Cover pot and simmer for approximately 30 minutes or until puffed up and done.

1 Tbsp. garlic oil (use oil left over after roasting garlic for the stock)
1 Tbsp. chopped parsley
1 Tbsp. chopped basil
1 cup boiling water
Sea salt & pepper to taste
2 eggs, separated
1 cup matzo meal
1 lg. celery stalk, chopped
1 clove garlic, chopped
1 sm. onion, grilled and chopped

*Savoring the Shore*

Meat from one whole turkey cooked as above

3 cloves garlic chopped

8 cloves of roasted garlic – roast in olive oil until soft and smoosh on a spoon and mix into stock - save the oil for matzo balls

3 large carrots, cut into small cubes

2 large onions, grilled and cut into small cubes

3 celery stalks, cut into small cubes

3 parsnips or turnips, cut into small cubes

2 beets cut into small cubes

1-1/2 quarts of your favorite vegetable chopped, mine is broccolini

1 recipe matzo balls  - you may use store mix and add additional herbs

2 Tbsp. fresh chopped parsley leaves

2 Tbsp. chopped chives

3 Tbsp. chopped basil leaves

1 tsp. red pepper flakes (gives a little kick – you may omit if you don't like spice)

## Soup:

Take the stock that you prepared and add the rest of the ingredients from 3 cloves garlic chopped through 1 tsp. red pepper flakes. While the soup is cooking, prepare matzo balls according to directions and cook in some of the stock. Set aside.

Ladle soup evenly onto 6 to 8 plates. Place 1 or 2 matzo balls in soup (depending on their size). Just before serving, add chopped parsley for garnish.

---

**Chef Marilyn Schlossbach** has been named one of the Best Chefs America 2013. She owns a number of restaurants at the NJ Shore including Langosta Lounge in Asbury Park and Labrador Lounge in Normandy Beach.

# Kom Kha Gai Soup (Thai Coconut Milk Soup)

*Connie Blumhardt, Publisher, Roast Magazine*

Serves 10

1 medium onion sliced thin

2 cans 14 oz. unsweetened coconut milk (I like to use a Thai brand)

2 cans 14 oz. chicken broth

2 lbs. mushrooms (doesn't matter what kind)

1.5 lbs. thinly sliced chicken breast

1 Tbsp. fish sauce

2 Tbsp. Sriracha or other chili sauce

2 Tbsp. finely chopped ginger

1 tsp. sugar

1/2 cup of cilantro

2 Tbsp. fresh lime juice

Salt and pepper to taste

In a saucepan, add sliced onion and cook until opaque, about 4 minutes. Add coconut milk, chicken broth, mushrooms and bring to a boil. Add chicken, fish sauce, chili sauce, ginger and sugar and cook on medium heat for 5-10 minutes, until chicken is cooked through. Add the lime juice and top with cilantro.

# Thai Chicken Soup

*Wakefern Food Corporation, ShopRite®, Lynn P. Logg, Corporate Chef*

*"This soup is very light and E-A-S-Y. Everything goes in the slow cooker!"*

Trim fat from chicken thighs. Cover and place in refrigerator.

For the soup, in a 4- to 6- quart slow cooker stir together celery, carrots, onion, garlic, jalapeno, soy sauce, fish sauce, ginger, vinegar and lime juice. Place chicken over vegetables. Add chicken broth.

Cover and cook on HIGH 4 hours or until chicken pulls apart easily with a fork. Reduce heat to LOW. Add cilantro, water chestnuts and coconut milk; stir to combine. Cook 30 minutes. Using 2 forks, shred chicken in slow cooker.

Meanwhile, in a saucepan prepare rice according to package directions. Keep warm.

Spoon rice into individual serving bowls and top with soup. If desired, garnish with more cilantro and scallions, and serve.

*\*Use caution when handling hot peppers. Wear disposable gloves or wash hands in hot, soapy water afterward.*

**Serves 6**

- 1-1/2 lbs. boneless, skinless chicken thighs
- 2 celery stalks, halved, sliced on a bias 1/4 inch thick
- 2 carrots, peeled, halved, cut on a bias 1/2-inch thick
- 1 medium onion, diced
- 3 garlic cloves, thinly sliced
- 1/2 jalapeno, seeds and veins removed, finely minced*
- 2 Tbsp. Kikkoman® Soy Sauce
- 2 Tbsp. fish sauce
- 2 Tbsp. peeled, grated fresh ginger
- 1-1/2 Tbsp. ShopRite® Red Wine Vinegar
- 1/4 cup fresh lime juice
- 2 qts. ShopRite® Reduced Sodium Chicken Broth
- 1/2 cup coarsely chopped fresh cilantro
- 1 (14 oz.) can sliced water chestnuts, drained
- 1/3 to 1/2 (14 oz.) can unsweetened coconut milk
- 1 cup basmati rice, uncooked
- Garnish (optional): Chopped fresh cilantro, thinly sliced scallions

*Savoring the Shore*

# Scrippelle 'MBusse (Crepes in Broth)

*Jillian Simone*

4 large eggs
2 Tbsp. milk
2 tsp. flour
1/4 cup Parmesan cheese + 1/2 cup set aside (used to sprinkle on cooked crepes before rolling)
Pinch of salt
Chicken broth
(we use 32 Oz. College Inn Broth)

Place eggs, milk, flour and 1/4 cup cheese in bowl and beat with whisk. Season with salt.

Heat a small crepe pan and rub bottom with butter or oil.

Add a scant one fourth cup batter, pouring off any excess, and cook crepe lightly on each side.

Grease pan after each crepe.

When all crepes are cooked, sprinkle one crepe at a time with additional Parmesan cheese and roll up very tightly.

Places two crepes in bottom of soup plate and spoon over piping hot chicken broth.

Jillian's grandparents first met in Atlantic City, NJ, when her grandfather was on leave during World War II. The rest, as they say, is history! Her family's love of the NJ shore has continued to this day with visits to Ocean City. *(Photo courtesy of the Simone family)*

*Soups and Sandwiches*

# Zuppa De Pesce
*Stars of HOPE*

Scrub & clean all shellfish thoroughly. Be especially careful to throw away any clams or mussels that don't close or stay closed.

Brown garlic in oil in large stock pot.

Place mussels and clams together in the pot. Pour in 1 to 2 cups of water. Bring to a boil and steam for about 15 minutes. Check to be sure all clams and mussels open if not let cook a little longer. When opened remove from pot and set aside. Discard any that do not open.

Add remaining ingredients and cover pot tightly. Simmer for 30 minute check and stir occasionally.

Add the clams & mussels back in and stir all together. Serve over linguini with fresh Italian bread and wine.

*You can also add lobster or crabs or both if you would like*

Mangia! Mangia! Enjoy!

1 (32 ounce) can crushed tomatoes
3 lbs. mussels
3 lbs. calamari
2 lbs. shrimp (cleaned)
2 lbs. scallops
8 garlic cloves
Red pepper flakes
Fresh parsley
Olive oil
Salt
Pepper
1 lb. pasta (linguini)

### Stars of HOPE

*"My mother-in-law, Debby Vincent owns and operates Assisted Living Homes for Disabled Veterans. In 2006, a tornado destroyed one of the homes and killed one of the veterans.* **New York Says Thank You** *came to Groesbeck, Texas in September 2007 and built a new home for my brother-in-law James Vincent and his family. It was a tremendous experience working with volunteers from New York and all over the country to build a house. It made me extremely proud to be an American and take part in a grassroots project to pay forward kindness. In December 2007, the founder of NYSTY asked us, the Vincent family, if we wanted to make wooden stars to take to Greensburg, Kansas, a town that was almost completely destroyed by an EF5 tornado. We jumped at the chance to "pay it forward" and made about 300 stars to take to Greensburg for the school kids there to paint messages of hope. These stars were then placed all over the devastated landscape of the small Kansas town.*

*This was the first of what became the Stars of HOPE project."* – *Pat Samuels, Program Director, Stars of HOPE,* **www.starsofhopeusa.org.**

# [First Discovered in] Nantucket Clam Chowder

*Sharon Roberts Karl*

1/2 lb. finely chopped bacon, I use some Hormel bits with melted butter
1 large onion
1 carrot, finely chopped
3/4 cup celery, minced
2 tsp. dried thyme
1 Tbsp. dried dill weed
1/2 tsp. white pepper
1/4 cup flour
3 cups clam juice or fish stock
1/2 cup dry white wine
3 (6.5 oz.) cans of minced clams, with juice
3 bay leaves
3 cups diced potatoes cooked till tender
1 cup heavy cream

**Shark River Inlet from Avon-By-The-Sea, NJ**

*"The house was built in the 1700's. There was a fireplace in every room. The kitchen had a full shelf of extremely old cook books. The 'Quahog (large clam) Chowder' page opened by itself from wear and is now a favorite in the Karl kitchen!" –Sharon Roberts Karl*

## The Base:

In a large heavy gauge stock pot cook the bacon over medium-high heat until the fat is rendered and the bacon is crisp. Add the onions, carrot, celery until the vegetables are tender, about 8 min. Add the thyme, dill weed and pepper and sauté 2 min. longer. Stir in the flour and cook, stirring constantly over low or medium heat for 4 to 6 min. Do not allow the flour to burn.

## The Chowder:

Heat the clam juice and wine with the bay leaves in a 2 quart non aluminum saucepan over high heat until boiling. Lower the heat and cook at a simmer for about 5 min. then gradually stir the broth into the base. Raise the heat under the stock pot to medium and cook the chowder for 10 min. stirring frequently. Add the clams and the potatoes. Roughly mash about 1/2 cup potatoes against the side of the pot and heat until the chowder is warmed through. At this point the chowder may be refrigerated for up to 3 days loosely-covered with plastic wrap.

To serve add heavy cream and allow the chowder to reheat to serving temperature, taking care not to let the mixture boil. Bay leaf may be removed before serving.

# Coastal Bouillabaisse

*Executive Chef Anthony Micari, The Ebbitt Room, Cape May*

## Saffron Orange Broth:

In a large sauce, pot heat oil over medium heat. Begin browning the lobster bodies and break them up with a spoon. Add in the onion, carrot, and celery and saute until the vegetables become aromatic. Next, add in the fennel and garlic and saute two more minutes. Add in the tomato paste and cook three minutes coating all of the vegetables with tomato. Deglaze with white wine, add in oranges, saffron and water and simmer for 45 minutes. Strain through a fine mesh strainer and chill.

3 Tbsp. blend oil
5 lbs. lobster bodies (rough chopped)
1 whole garlic bulb
1 onion (julienne)
3 heads fennel (julienne)
1 bunch celery (rough chop)
2 carrots (peeled and rough chop)
3 oranges (cut in half)
1 qt. white wine
1 Tbsp. saffron
3 qt. water
1 cup tomato paste

## Garlic Mayo:

In a food processor add in the roasted garlic cloves, egg yolks, paprika, mustard and begin to blend smooth. Add in the lemon juice and then slowly add in the oil until the mixture becomes smooth and firm. Season with salt and pepper and reserve.

1 whole bulb garlic (roasted)
1 cup lemon juice
1 Tbsp. paprika
1 Tbsp. mustard
3 egg yolks
1 cup canola oil

## To Assemble:

In a saute pan, heat olive oil and begin searing the shrimp and scallops. Add in the garlic and shallots and then the shellfish and squid. Deglaze with the saffron orange broth, cover and simmer for 5 minutes.

3 oz fresh squid
8 littleneck clams
10 mussels
3 U 10 (size) scallops
2 U 12 (size) shrimp
2 Tbsp. chiffonade parsley
1 Tbsp. garlic minced
1 Tbsp. shallot minced
2 Tbsp. olive oil
Salt and pepper to taste
1.5 qt. saffron orange broth

## While that is Simmering:

Grill a slice of your favorite crusty bread with olive oil, salt and pepper. Uncover the bouillabaisse and place in a large bowl. Top with grilled bread and the drizzle with the garlic mayo and serve.

Executive Chef Anthony Micari has been named to Best Chefs America 2013.

*Savoring the Shore*

**Chef Anthony Micari (left) Executive Chef of The Ebbitt Room and Chef Jeremy Einhorn Executive Chef of the Blue Pig Tavern in Cape May pick fresh produce for their tables at Beach Plum Farm in West Cape May.**

*(Photo courtesy Beach Plum Farm)*

## About The Virginia Hotel and The Ebbitt Room:

*The Virginia, Cape May's foremost luxury hotel, offers luxurious accommodations and personalized service in an immaculately restored 1879 landmark building, reopened by Curtis Bashaw of Cape Resorts Group in 1989. Featuring 24 well-appointed guestrooms, intimate public spaces like the lobby bar and enclosed sun porches, and The Ebbitt Room – the hotel's signature restaurant, The Virginia offers its adult-only guests a flawless integration of service and style with a timeless glamour. The Ebbitt Room provides its discerning visitors with seasonal farm-to-table offerings from Beach Plum Farm, bringing the fresh food movement forward in Cape May. Recently acknowledged by Condé Nast Traveler in the 2012 Reader's Choice Awards as a top hotel in the Northeast, as well as in the magazine's prestigious 2013 Gold List, the hotel is nestled on Jackson Street in the heart of the famed historic district of Cape May, New Jersey, and is mere half block from the town's beautiful beaches. Web site: www.virginiahotel.com.*

*Soups and Sandwiches*

# Bouillabaisse

*Betsy Belt*

In a large kettle heat oil, celery, onion, garlic, leek, thyme and bay leaf and cook five minutes.

Add tomatoes, clam juice, wine, fennel, salt, pepper, and parsley and simmer 15 minutes.

Add seafood and cook fifteen minutes longer. All clam and mussel shells should be open at this point, otherwise discard. YUM!

Serves six

1/4 cup olive oil
1 stalk celery
1 medium onion chopped
1 clove garlic minced
1 leek diced
1/2 tsp thyme
1/2 bay leaf
2 cups chopped fresh Roma tomatoes
1 cup bottle clam juice
1 cup dry white wine
1/4 cup chopped fresh fennel or
   1/2 tsp crushed fennel seeds
Salt and pepper to taste
2 Tbsp. chopped parsley
1 lobster cut into pieces
12 clams
12 mussels, scrubbed and debearded
12 raw shrimp, shelled and deveined
12 scallops
1 lb. red snapper or cod, cut into
   serving size pieces

# Prawn and Sausage Gumbo

*Sarah Pritchard, PritchardPhotography@Live.com*

**For the roux:**

In a large heavy sauce pan or Dutch oven combine flour and oil. Mix until smooth. Cook over high heat for 5 minutes, stirring constantly. Cook and stir for 10 minutes on medium heat. The roux will turn reddish.

Stir in onion, celery, green pepper, garlic, red peppers and black pepper. Cook over medium heat for 3 – 5 minutes or until vegetables are crisp-tender, stirring often. Gradually stir in hot chicken broth, sausage and bay leaves. Bring to a boil then reduce heat. Cover and simmer 20 – 30 minutes. Discard bay leaves.

Add fresh prawns for the last 5 minutes of cooking. Serve over the rice.

1/3 cup flour
1/4 cup cooking oil
1/2 cup chopped onion
1/3 cup chopped celery
1/3 cup chopped green pepper
4 cloves garlic, minced
1/4 tsp. ground red pepper
Black pepper to taste
3 cups chicken broth, heated
8 oz. smoked sausage cut into
   bite-sized cubes
2 bay leaves
1 lb. prawns (shrimp)
   cleaned and deveined
Hot cooked rice

# Grilled Sweet Jersey Corn Chowder

*Chef Amanda Giblin, Hell's Kitchen Season 11*

Prep time: 25 min.
Total Cook time: 60 min.
Yields: 8 cups

2 Tbsp. extra virgin olive oil
4 oz. bacon; diced
1 large Spanish onion; diced
2 ea. leeks; washed,
white parts only
sliced into half circles
4 stalks celery, diced
1 large red bell pepper
1 large green bell pepper
3 Tbsp. unsalted butter
4 Tbsp. A.P. (All Purpose) flour
8 cups corn stock
(recipe to follow)
2 large Idaho potatoes,
peeled and diced
Grilled corn kernels
1 tsp. Tabasco sauce
Salt and pepper to taste

Husk your fresh corn, rinsing away the silk hairs. Season with olive oil, salt and pepper. Place on a hot grill. Cook until corn becomes brown and starts to crackle. When cool enough to handle, CAREFULLY cut the corn off the Cobb. Set aside. (CHEF TIP: It is easiest to place the flat or bottom part of the corn on the cutting board and cut from pointe tip to base.)

In a medium stock pot, place your corn cobs, vegetable OR chicken stock, 36% cream, bundled thyme, onion, celery, garlic, and salt. Bring to boil then immediately reduce to a simmer. Allow flavors to meld for 30 min. Strain and set aside.

Using the same pot, on medium high heat, add oil and sauté bacon until almost crispy (2-3 min). Add onion, leeks, celery, and bell peppers and continue to sauté until onions become translucent. Add butter and let it melt completely. Sprinkle in flour. Using a whisk, allow flour and butter to form a roux. (CHEF TIP: Your roux should look like wet beach sand.) Let the roux cook the flour flavor out. You'll know when this step is complete because your roux will have a nutty aroma. Using a ladle, gradually whisk in the corn stock.

## Corn Stock:

4-6 ears of fresh sweet Jersey corn
4 cups vegetable stock OR
chicken stock
6 cups 36% heavy cream
2 oz. fresh thyme; bundled in
butchers twine
1 large onion; chopped
3 stalks celery, washed and chopped
6 each garlic clove, whole
2 tsp. kosher salt

Add potatoes, grilled corn kernels, and Tabasco sauce. Simmer, uncovered for another 30 min. or until potatoes are tender. Season with salt and pepper to your desired taste.

*©ChefAmandaGiblin, reprinted with permission*

**Chef Amanda Giblin** competed on Hell's Kitchen Season 11 on the Fox Network. She is originally from New Jersey. Her shore towns are Tom's River, Seaside Heights and Seaside Park.

# Grilled Portobello Peach Sandwiches

*Dianne Wenz, Vegan Health and Lifestyle Coach, www.veggiegirl.com*

*"These Portobello peach sandwiches are perfect for summertime cookouts at the shore or in your backyard. Mushrooms and peaches both grill really quickly, so dinner will be ready before you know it." – Dianne Wenz*

Combine the pesto ingredients in a food processor fitted with an s-blade. Process until ingredients are chopped and just slightly chunky, scraping down bowl with a rubber spatula if necessary. If the pesto seems too dry, add a little more oil, one tablespoon at a time. Store in the refrigerator until ready to use.

Mix all of the marinade ingredients together in a small bowl. Place the mushrooms in a flat baking dish and pour the marinade over them. If your mushrooms are really large you may need to double the marinade recipe. Let the mushrooms sit for an hour or two.

Lightly oil and heat the grill. Place the mushrooms and onions on the grill and let cook between 10 to 15 minutes, until tender, flipping halfway through. The peaches only need 5 to 8 minutes to cook, so place them on the grill when you flip the mushrooms and onions. Flip them halfway through as well. Grill the bread for a minute or two, if you wish.

Assemble the sandwiches by spreading the spinach pesto on the roll, then layering on a mushroom, onion slice, half a peach and one or two tomato slices. I like to serve my sandwiches with a side salad and grilled corn on the cob.

## Sandwich Ingredients:

4 large portobello mushrooms, cleaned
2 ripe peaches, sliced in half and pitted
1 sweet onion, sliced
4 rolls (the more rustic and "hearty" the bread, the better), sliced
1 thinly sliced tomato
Spinach pesto (recipe follows)

## Mushroom Marinade:

1/4 cup olive oil
2 Tbsp. lemon juice
1 Tbsp. soy sauce
1 sprig fresh rosemary
1/2 tsp. sea salt
1/2 tsp. black pepper
2 cloves garlic, minced

## Spinach Pesto:

5 oz. baby spinach – about 4 cups
1/8 cup extra virgin olive oil
1/4 cup nuts (pine nuts are traditional, but walnuts and cashews work nicely with this recipe too)
2 garlic cloves
2 tsp. lemon juice
1/2 tsp. sea salt

*Savoring the Shore*

# Weeknight Pizza Margherita
*Kate Kurelja*

1 - 28 oz. can whole San Marzano
tomatoes
Extra virgin olive oil
Salt and pepper
6 oz. fresh mozzarella
Fresh basil
Pizza dough

Special equipment:
pizza stone, pizza peel

*"A delicious meal made easy for weeknights with a simple cheat - premade dough. Many pizza places will sell a ball of dough, or check your local supermarket. I like to use whole wheat for a healthier and slightly chewier alternative." –Kate Kurelja*

Preheat the oven to 500 degrees F. When the oven reaches temperature, add the pizza stone. Let the stone heat for 20 minutes. Meanwhile, add the tomatoes and juice to a blender. Pulse to blend, stop while the tomatoes are still red. Lightly flour the pizza peel. Gently stretch and pull the dough to cover the peel. Ladle about 1/2 cup of tomato sauce onto the dough. (Freeze the rest for next week!). Sprinkle fresh ground salt and pepper over the tomato sauce, then drizzle with 1-2 Tbsp. of extra virgin olive oil. Thinly slice 4-6 oz. of mozzarella and spread evenly over the tomato sauce. Top generously with fresh basil leaves. Open the oven and position the peel over the (very) hot stone. Carefully slide the pizza off of the peel and onto the stone. Bake until golden brown and bubbling, about 10-12 minutes.

# Pulled Chicken Sliders
*Cheryl Larkin*

Serves 4

One store bought roasted
rotisserie chicken
1 – 2 bottles favorite barbeque sauce
(consider white barbeque sauce)
Salt and pepper
One package slider rolls
(we like whole grain)
One large fresh tomato, sliced
Fresh washed lettuce slices
1/2 lb. deli coleslaw

Remove and discard skin and bones from chicken. Shred chicken meat using two forks to pull apart. Place in slow cooker pot if available and turn on warm. Season with salt and pepper. Pour one bottle of barbeque sauce over top and cover pot. Warm through (may be warmed through in pan on stove, stir occasionally to prevent sticking). Serve on slider rolls topped with sliced tomato and lettuce or with coleslaw. Serve additional barbeque sauce on the side.

# Chicken Quesadillas
*Sarah Caldwell*

4 servings

8 small flour tortillas
1 rotisserie chicken shredded
1 onion thinly sliced
1 green pepper thinly sliced
1 cup of sliced mushrooms
2 cups shredded cheddar cheese
2 Tbsp. Cajun seasoning
(In NJ and NYC we use Dinosaur
Bar-B-Que Cajun Foreplay
Spice Rub)
Olive oil

Cook onions, green peppers and mushrooms in a frying pan with 1 Tbsp. of olive for 5 min or until onions are transparent. Set aside. Thinly coat a frying pan with olive oil and place on medium/high heat.

Place 1 tortilla in the frying pan and sprinkle with Cajun seasoning. Layer cheese, vegetables, chicken, cheese and Cajun seasoning in that order followed by a flour tortilla on top. Cook for 3 minutes or until first layer of cheese is melted. Flip quesadilla and cook for 3 more minutes or until all cheese is melted and tortillas are golden brown. Remove from heat and keep warm until ready to serve. To serve, cut each quesadilla into 6 pieces and serve with your favorite dressings such as sour cream, guacamole and salsa.

# Real Philly Cheesesteak

*Heather L. McCurdy, www.realthekitchenandbeyond.com*

*"I'm a Philly girl and we are really particular about our cheese steaks. My family has been known to [argue] discuss what a REAL cheese steak is. My dad would have to be the expert since he is Philly born and raised but sometimes he adds mushrooms to his and I am sorry but let's be real, it isn't REAL. Today let's talk about how to make a cheese steak.*

*So you will tell me mine aren't real either because there is one thing I refuse to use – Cheez Whiz, well, two since I won't use American on mine either – the kids can have it. I prefer provolone or just a pinch of cheddar, extra sharp.*

*But that isn't where it all starts. It starts with a roll. A good roll. A long hard roll…. Now that you bought your rolls, make sure you have good beef. None of that Steak'um freezer stuff. You have to have REAL thin sliced or chip steak – preferably chipped since the thin slice can still be chunky and so not right. The other thing you want to do is make sure it's GOOD beef – grass fed beef is a winner in our house. Lower fat and higher flavor. Can't lose…"*
– Heather L. McCurdy, **www.realthekitchenandbeyond.com**

Melt 2 tablespoons of butter in a cast iron skillet. Thinly slice 3 onions length wise and start frying.

When the onions are almost done, start cooking the beef in the same pan (if everyone likes onions). Cook the beef just until it is no longer pink. Keep it juicy and just done. Push the onions and meat to the side of the pan and slap an opened roll open side down in the pan to brown a little. Once the roll is done add a little mayonnaise, or a lot. Pile on the onions if cooked separately, then the cheese, then the meat (or meat and onions together if cooked together). Pile it on until the roll barely closes. Pair with an ice cold Coke (in a bottle) or a pale ale. Perfection!

2 Tbsp. butter
3 medium onions
1 lb. chip steak
5 six-inch steak rolls
Cheese
Mayonnaise

*"Growing up the oldest of 7 in a not so well off family, we didn't really go on vacation. One of the few vacations I remember was going to Cape May to visit my grandparents. We would arrive and the first thing we would do is look up, up, up - 6 floors to be exact - which seemed so high to us country kids. Floor 6, Victorian Towers, was where my grandparents lived. I remember being amazed to see the curtain move - my grandmother was watching for us to get there - the end of our 8 hour journey before cell phones meant she must have been checking often. They would buy us Cracker Jacks, Dots, Twizzlers, and marshmallow cones. We would go to the beach early enough that you didn't need the newly instituted beach tag, visit the bunker, gathering pearly iridescent shells, then struggle to then slow down and listen as my almost blind grandfather would catch sounds and stop us to listen, to be still. Inevitably we would end up at Sunset Beach to marvel at the concrete ship slowly disappearing. The final trip would be the Cape May Zoo. We always knew we were almost there when we saw THE white horse. Today I take my kids to Cape May and try to bottle up the past. Try to give them just a little taste of those irreplaceable memories with my grandparents."*
–Heather L. McCurdy

*Savoring the Shore*

# Whiskey Jersey Burgers

*Ben Carothers and Patrick Rutherford*

Makes 4 burgers

1 lb. ground beef
1 Tbsp. ground black pepper
1 Tbsp. garlic salt
5 Tbsp. (Tennessee whiskey or Bourbon)
4 slices cheddar cheese
4 slices pork roll
4 buns

Preheat grill to 400 degrees F or medium heat.

Hand mix ground beef, pepper, salt and whiskey in a mixing bowl. Prepare 4 hamburger patties from the seasoned ground beef. Place patties on grill and cook to preference (4-5 minutes on each side for well-done hamburgers). With roughly 30 seconds to 1 minute remaining in cooking, place one slice of cheese on each patty for melting. Grill pork roll until each side is crisp. Place the prepared patties on a bun and top with the prepared pork roll.

*Taylor Ham (brand name) or generically pork roll are processed pork products. According to* **Karen Schnitzspahn** *author of* **Jersey Shore Food History Victorian Feasts to Boardwalk Treats,** *the product was first introduced as a retail food item by a NJ businessman, John Taylor of Trenton, NJ, who formed the Taylor Provision Company in 1888. At one time there were a number of Taylor Ham stores at the NJ Shore.*

# Blue Cheese, Prosciutto and Arugula Bruschetta

*Guillaume and Jennifer Schmittheisler*

1 large store-bought bruschetta or 4 individual-size bruschetta
1/3 cup extra virgin olive oil
1 clove garlic, halved
2 Tbsp. balsamic vinegar
3 oz. arugula
4 slices Prosciutto
4 oz. crumbled blue cheese
1/8 cup chopped nuts (walnuts, pecans, hazelnuts or similar)

Brush bruschetta with 1 tbsp. olive oil and grill each side for one minute or until golden. Then rub one side with garlic. If using large bruschetta, cut into four slices. Arrange Prosciutto on garlic-rubbed side of bruschetta. Whisk together remaining olive oil with balsamic vinegar. Toss arugula with half of dressing then arrange on Prosciutto. Sprinkle with blue cheese and nuts.

Adapted from "Blue Cheese, Prosciutto and Rocket Bruschetta," by Valli Little, Taste.com.au, News Limited, November 2004.

*"My family and I have been coming to Lavallette since I was born. It has been and will always be a special place for us. Now married, my husband and I look forward to building more memories with our future family. We want to thank everyone that has participated in the [Sandy] relief effort. We wouldn't be able to build more memories if it weren't for your hard work and sacrifice." –Jennifer Schmittheisler*

# Grilled Brie Sandwiches

*Cheryl Larkin*

1/2 loaf French bread, thinly sliced
1/2 lb. Brie, thinly sliced, white rind removed if preferred
Apricot preserves (we like all fruit)
Butter

Spread one slice of French bread with apricot jam and top with a thin layer of Brie and a second slice of French bread lightly buttered on the outside. Place in a heated frying pan or on a grill pan buttered side down and carefully butter the top slice of bread. Cook over medium high heat turning once until golden brown on both sides.

Salads and Sides

Savoring the Shore

# Insalata di Arance

*Chef Joe Introna, Joe Leone's, Point Pleasant Beach and Sea Girt, NJ*

6 oranges, 5 oz. each
Blood oranges or regular oranges
3 oz. red onion, julienned
4 oz. cured black olives, pitted
12 oz. baby arugula lettuce or
spinach, washed and dried
TT (To Taste) coarse salt
TT cracked black pepper
TT extra virgin olive oil

First segment the oranges then slice the red onion julienne. Then toss the oranges, onions, arugula or spinach and olives together in a bowl. Next season the salad with salt and black pepper. Lastly drizzle with extra virgin olive oil and serve.

## St. Joseph and Our Community

*"St. Joseph is known in history as a worker and a helper. He was known to lend a hand when others were in need and he exemplified this type of behavior during his lifetime. As our community works hard to rebuild itself from the devastation of Super Storm Sandy, I am continually reminded of St. Joseph and his good works. I feel he would have wanted to help our community get back on its feet and become stronger than ever. With this sentiment in mind, I have submitted two recipes that we offer in celebration of St Joseph's Day to pay tribute to St. Joseph for his guidance and to ask for his blessing as we rebuild our community.*

*As St. Joseph is my patron Saint, we honor him by celebrating two feast days for him: one on March 19th for St. Joseph the Husband of Mary and the second on May 1st for St. Joseph the Worker.*

*I am sharing…two recipes with you [this and St. Joseph's Day Cruller Pastry] because we traditionally eat them on both of the St. Joseph's Feast days. The Insalata di Arance is one of my favorite St. Joseph's day treats, and the St. Joseph's Cruller Pastry is another favorite enjoyed by many during St. Joseph's Day Celebrations.*

*I hope that through the strength of our community working together and the blessings from St. Joseph, all those affected by Super Storm Sandy will rebuild and come back stronger than ever."*

*– Chef Joe Introne*

*(Facing page photo courtesy Beach Plum Farm, Cape May, NJ. This page photos courtesy Joe Leone's, Point Pleasant Beach and Sea Girt, NJ)*

*Salads and Sides*

# Apple Fennel Spinach Salad

*Anna Linn Currie*

Mix from zest down in a bowl or lidded container. Toss the salad with the dressing. Eat and enjoy.

1 bag spinach
1/2 large fennel bulb thinly sliced
1/2 green apple match sticks
1 tsp. orange zest
1/8 cup orange juice
1 small shallot minced
1/8 cup cider, red wine, or champagne vinegar
1/8 cup olive oil (add more to taste)
Pinch of kosher salt

# Bok Choy Salad

*Mary Lyons*

*"This is easy and healthy! Great for potlucks too!" – Mary Lyons*

Brown sesame seeds, almonds and ramen noodles in oil. Cool. Add to Bok Choy in large bowl.

### Dressing:

Heat 1/2 cup sugar, 1/2 cup cider vinegar and 2 Tbsp. soy sauce to dissolve. Cool. Add to Bok Choy right before serving.

1 head chopped Bok Choy (leaves and stalk)
1/4 cup canola oil
1/2 cup sesame seeds
1/2 cup sliced almonds
2 packages uncooked ramen noodles, crumbled. Discard seasoning packet.

# Napa Cabbage Salad

*Laura Currie*

### Dressing:

Combine all of the above by whisking together.

### Salad:

In a large salad bowl, place the salad ingredients and dressing and toss until evenly distributed. Enjoy!!

Adapted from *Cooking Thin with Chef Kathleen* by Kathleen Daelemans

1 Tbsp. sesame oil
3 Tbsp. rice wine vinegar
1/4 cup soy sauce (I use low sodium)
1 Tbsp. sugar
1 tsp. freshly grated ginger or 1/2 tsp. dried ginger

1 head of napa cabbage washed, dried and sliced
1 cup loosely packed cilantro leaves
2-3 scallions, thinly sliced (white and green parts)
1 medium carrot, grated

*Savoring the Shore*

# Broccoli Slaw

*Dianne Wenz, Vegan Health and Lifestyle Coach, www.veggiegirl.com*

1 bunch broccoli, cut into small, bite-sized florets
2 carrots, shredded
1/4 red onion, diced
1/4 cup vegan mayonnaise
1 Tbsp. yellow mustard
1/2 avocado, mashed
1/4 tsp. garlic powder
1/4 tsp. sea salt
1/4 tsp. black pepper
Sesame seeds

*"Cole slaw is quintessentially Jersey to me, as it always conjures up images of late night trips to the diner for a club sandwich with a side of fries. This broccoli slaw is a healthy twist on the diner classic, and is the perfect side dish for your summer time cookout."*
*– Dianne Wenz*

Using a steamer basket in a pot of shallow water or an electric steamer, steam the broccoli for a few minutes until bright green and firm-crisp. If you don't have a steamer basket, you can lightly steam the broccoli covered in a shallow pan with a little water. You can use raw broccoli, but it's harder to digest raw. Rinse the broccoli in cold water.

In a small bowl, mix together the mayo, avocado, garlic powder, sea salt and black pepper.

Place the carrots, broccoli and onion in a large bowl, add the dressing and mix well. Top with sesame seeds. Refrigerate for a few hours or overnight, to allow the flavors to combine. Serve chilled.

*(Photo courtesy www.veggiegirl.com)*

# Spinach Pesto Salad

*Cheryl Larkin*

Serves 4 to 6

One 9 oz. bag fresh spinach
One cup frozen peas, defrosted
1/2 cup prepared basil pesto (from 8 oz. store bought jar, or homemade), add more to taste
1/2 cup shredded (not grated) Parmesan cheese
1/4 cup pignoli nuts (pine nuts), toasted

Combine spinach and defrosted peas in a salad bowl. Toss with basil pesto. Add shredded Parmesan cheese and toasted Pignoli nuts. Toss lightly to combine. (To toast pignoli nuts place on a piece of foil in a toaster oven or under the broiler for about 2 – 3 minutes. Watch closely and remove as soon as they turn light golden – otherwise they will quickly burn.)

Adapted from Ina Garten's Pesto Pea Salad, 2004

# Kale and Fuji Apple Slaw

*Kate Strangfeld, Icing off the Cake, www.icingoffthecake.com*

*"This light and refreshing slaw is a perfect late spring/summer side salad or potluck dish. In the past year or two, kale has dominated both restaurant menus and cooking magazines. As you probably already know, it's a nutritional powerhouse and has a bit more "oomph" than other greens like spinach. Here, it adds body and texture, without being too overpowering. The key to toning down kale's bitter and strong flavor is to "massage" it with the dressing.*

*While the number of recipes with kale has exploded, I've yet to see one with an Asian twist. Adding miso adds a tang that compliments the rest of the slaw beautifully."*
*– Kate Strangfeld*

Serves 6-8

3 Tbsp. miso paste
2 Tbsp. lemon juice
1 Tbsp. rice vinegar
1 to 2 Tbsp. extra virgin
   olive oil
2 bunches dinosaur kale, shredded*
2 apples, julienned
1/4 cup sliced almonds

*(Photo courtesy of www.icingoffthecake.com)*

Combine miso paste, lemon juice, rice vinegar, and oil in a medium bowl. Add in kale and apple and toss to thoroughly coat with dressing. Lightly massage the kale with your hands for about a minute. Place in fridge and let sit for at least an hour for flavors to marinate into kale then serve. This slaw is great for leftovers; it will last for about four to five days in the fridge.

*\*For best and quickest results, shred the kale with a food processor (use the shredding attachment) and julienne the apple with a mandoline. If you don't have a food processor or mandoline, use a knife.*

**Kate Strangfeld** is a former NJ resident who has packed a lot of food experience into a few short years. As explained on her blog, www.icingoffthecake.com, her love affair with food kicked into high gear at the Natural Gourmet Institute for Culinary Arts and Health in Manhattan from which she graduated. She recently has worked at the *Yale Rudd Center for Food Policy and Obesity* and for First Lady Michelle Obama's *Let's Move! initiative.*

*Savoring the Shore*

# NJ Peach and Burrata Salad

*Executive Chef Jeremy Einhorn, Blue Pig Tavern, Congress Hall Hotel, Cape May NJ*

Serves 4

2 each burrata, 4oz balls
2 ripe NJ peaches, medium dice
1 pint heirloom cherry tomatoes,
cut in half, or quarters
1 pint blackberries, cut in half
8 slices prosciutto, sliced very thin
1 cup baby arugula,
washed and dried
3 Tbsp. extra virgin olive oil
salt and pepper to taste
1 Tbsp. sugar

*(Photo courtesy of Beach Plum Farm, Cape May, NJ)*

Toss the peaches with the sugar and some salt and pepper. Meanwhile, heat a pan over high heat with 2 tbsp of olive oil.

Quickly sauté the peaches to lightly soften and caramelize the sugar. Be careful not to overcook the peaches.

Arrange the peaches, tomatoes and blackberries on the bottom of the plate. Then place the prosciutto around the plate.

Carefully cut the burrata into quarters. Place around the plate. Drizzle with Extra Virgin Olive Oil and garnish with the baby arugula.

# Flume Salad Dressing

*Debby Larkin*

1/8 cup sugar (or less)
1/4 cup red wine vinegar
1/4 cup ketchup
2 Tbsp. salad oil
2 Tbsp. diced celery
2 Tbsp. diced green pepper
1 Tbsp. minced onion
1 tsp. salt (or to taste)
Pepper (to taste)
Fresh garlic

*This is the house dressing recipe from The Flume restaurant on Cape Cod which closed many years ago." – Debby Larkin*

Combine all ingredients in a jar with a good seal. Add one ice cube and shake ingredients till ice cube is completely melted. Refrigerate.

# Butter Lettuce with Apples, Walnuts, and Pomegranate Seeds

*Chef Robert Aikens, The Peacock, Manhattan, suggested by Betsy Belt*

## For Vinaigrette

Whisk first 4 ingredients in a medium bowl. Gradually whisk in oil. Season vinaigrette to taste with salt and pepper.

## For Salad:

Place lettuce in a large bowl. Add vinaigrette, walnuts, and apple, toss to coat. Season with salt and pepper. Garnish with pomegranate seeds, tarragon, and cheese.

Prior to arriving in New York for the upcoming opening of The Peacock, British born **Chef Robert Aikens** has most recently been affiliated with Dandelion in Philadelphia.

## About The Peacock:

*With Jason Hicks of Jones Wood Foundry and Yves Jadot of Raines Law Room at its helm, The Peacock will evoke an early 19th century English gentleman's club brought into the present with a playful Bohemian touch. There will be three components to the restaurant: a library bar and lounge complete with tall bookcases, club chairs and an open fire where hors d'oeuvres and high tea will be served, plus classic cocktails; and two adjoining dining rooms where a seasonal sophisticated menu inspired by classic British cuisine will be offered. An intimate outdoor terrace and private garden will complement the dining rooms, where guests can linger al fresco. Located beneath The Peacock with its own separate entrance from the street, The Shakespeare Pub will be emblematic of a 16th century pub found in Stratford upon Avon (Jason Hicks's hometown). Featuring stone floors, semi-private booths and quirky details married with simple English pub grub, cask ales and wines, The Shakespeare will lend a relaxed atmosphere for lunch and a pint by day and evolve into a vibrant bar by night.*
*– 24 East 39th Street, New York, NY*

4 Servings
2 Tbsp. cider vinegar
1 Tbsp. honey
1 Tbsp. finely chopped shallot
1-1/2 tsp. Dijon mustard
1/3 cup olive oil
Kosher salt and freshly ground
   pepper

2 heads of butter lettuce leaves,
   gently torn
1 cup store-bought glazed walnuts
1 Honeycrisp or Fuji apple, quartered,
   cored and thinly sliced
Kosher salt and fresh ground pepper
1 cup pomegranate seeds
1/4 cup tarragon leaves
1/2 cup crumbled Stilton or Maytag
   blue cheese (about 2 ounces)

# Orzo Salad

*Anna Schneider*

*"Nothing fancy but a great summer side dish, very easy & delicious." – Anna Schneider*

Cook & drain orzo & while still warm, add remaining ingredients. Mix well, refrigerate and serve.

2 cups uncooked orzo (1/2 box)
1 bottle Newman's oil & vinegar
   dressing
1/2 cup Parmesan cheese
1 cup red & green pepper diced
1/2 cup red onion diced
1 cup grape tomatoes halved

*Savoring the Shore*

# Quick Quinoa Salad

*Wendy Bright-Fallon, Renew Wellness (www.renewwellness.net), Red Bank, NJ*

Serves 4-6, gluten free, vegan
1 cup dry quinoa (color options: tan, red or black)
1-3/4 cup water (you can use veggie or chicken broth for added flavor)
1/2 tsp. sea salt

## Prepare Quinoa:

Rinse quinoa and drain (this is a very important step because it neutralizes the saponins that are bitter tasting and disrupt digestion). Bring rinsed quinoa, salt and water to a boil. Reduce heat to low, cover and simmer for 15-20 minutes (until water is fully absorbed). Uncover and fluff with fork.

## Salad:

Add above ingredients to prepared quinoa. Mix well.

1 carrot, chopped
1/3 cup parsley, minced
1-15 oz. can chickpeas or black beans, drained and rinsed
1/4 cup combination of toasted sunflower seeds, walnuts and/or pumpkin seeds
2-3 large handfuls of green of choice – you can use any green you like: spinach, kale, broccoli…
Handful of diced dried cherries (no sugar added), diced OR sun dried tomatoes

*(Photo courtesy of Nourish)*

## Dressing:

3-4 cloves garlic, minced
1/3 cup freshly squeezed lemon juice
1/4 cup organic olive oil
1-2 Tbsp. tamari

Whisk together ingredients and pour dressing over quinoa. Toss well. Serve at room temp or chilled.

*Variation:* Replace the tamari with ume plum vinegar but use less, try two teaspoons to start. Add more if needed. Stir well.

*"'I love how Rebecca Wood describes quinoa in her book The New Whole Foods Encyclopedia: "When cooked, the wispy germ separates from the seed, and its delicate – almost crunchy – curlicue makes a great visual and textural contrast to the soft grain.' Quinoa is a complete protein and rich in lysine - an amino acid not often found in a plant- based diet." –Wendy Bright-Fallon*

**Wendy Bright-Fallon** and **Debbie Peterson** are creators of the community-based cookbook *Nourish*.

# Sunflower Seed "Tuna" Salad

*Dianne Wenz, Vegan Health and Lifestyle Coach, www.veggiegirl.com*

*"This sunflower seed "tuna" salad is perfect for a day at the shore, as it travels well and there's no need to worry about eggy mayonnaise going bad in the sun. It's delcious on its own, works well in salads and is wonderful in sandwiches."*
*–Dianne Wenz*

## For the Salad:

1 cups raw sunflower seeds, soaked for four hours, dried and then ground in a food processor
3 celery stalk, finely diced
2 scallions, finely diced
2 tsp. dulse or kelp flakes
1/4 cup fresh dill, chopped

1/2 cups coconut water
2 cloves garlic
1/3 cup lemon juice
1 tsp. sea salt
3/4 cup raw cashews
3 Tbsp. stone ground mustard

## For the Mayo:

In a large mixing bowl, combine all of the salad ingredients. Toss to mix thoroughly.

In a high speed blender, combine all of the mayo ingredients and blend thoroughly.

Pour the dressing over the salad and toss to mix well.

*(Photo courtesy of www.veggiegirl.com)*

*Savoring the Shore*

# Red Potato and Dill Salad

*Wegmans Food Markets, Trent O'Drain, New Jersey Division Executive Chef*

2-1/2 lbs. Food You Feel Good About Red Potatoes, skin-on, 3/4-inch dice

1/4 cup chopped fresh dill

1 bunch green onions, trimmed, thinly sliced

1 cup Wegmans Plain Greek Yogurt

3-1/2 Tbsp. Wegmans Dijon Whole Grain Mustard

2 tsp. Italian Classics Hot Pepper Spread

Salt and pepper to taste

Add potatoes and enough cold water to cover stockpot. Simmer on MED about 20 min. (don't boil), until potatoes are fork-tender. Drain.

Arrange potatoes in a single layer on baking sheet. Cool 10 min.

Combine potatoes, dill, onion, yogurt, mustard and hot pepper spread in large mixing bowl. Season with salt and pepper.

*It was 1916 when brothers Walter and Jack Wegman began to sell produce from a pushcart wagon in the streets of Rochester, New York. This was the humble beginning of Wegmans Food Markets, still family-owned today, but now with 81 stores in six states. By the early 90s, Wegmans had expanded its reach beyond its home in New York State with a store in Erie, Pennsylvania and a plan to open more PA stores and eventually enter the New Jersey market.*

*Wegmans believed they could bring a unique shopping experience to New Jersey consumers, one that didn't already exist, combining incredible customer service, the best ingredients, help with meals, restaurant-quality prepared foods, and consistent low prices.*

*Selective in choosing sites, Wegmans scoured the state for ideal locations. The first store opened in 1999 in Princeton. By 2006, with the opening of the Cherry Hill store, there were seven Wegmans Food Markets in New Jersey. In 2001 and 2004, stores opened in Manalapan and Ocean.*

# A Taste of Miss America History from Atlantic City
*The Miss America Organization*

In 1921, tourists and locals flocked to the boardwalk in Atlantic City, New Jersey to witness King Neptune announce the winner of the Inter-City Beauty Contest; a contest that would transform into one of the most watched television programs in history. The Miss America Competition, which began as an idea to keep tourists at the Jersey Shore beyond Labor Day, became an annual tradition that would cherish the style, scholarship, service, and success of young females from across the nation. Since the crowning of Margaret Gorman, the first Miss America, in 1921, the Miss America Organization has endured significant changes, all of which have contributed to the success in creating a larger than life spectacle for people of all ages to enjoy. A successful event that has become an incredible part of the Miss America Competition each year involves a most beloved wardrobe accessory for many of the contestants... shoes.

*Savoring the Shore*

# Broccoli Casserole

*Miss America 2013 Mallory Hagan*

1 7 oz. can Green Giant Shoepeg
Corn
1 can cream of mushroom soup
1 small container sour cream
1 cup grated sharp cheddar cheese
1 package (small) frozen broccoli –
cooked
1 Tbsp. mayonnaise
1 can water chestnuts - chopped
1 tube Ritz crackers - crushed
1 stick margarine

Mix all ingredients except Ritz crackers, margarine and 1/4 of water chestnuts. Pour into small, greased casserole dish. Mix crushed Ritz crackers, 1/4 of water chestnuts, and margarine. Sprinkle over top of casserole. Bake at 350° for 30 minutes or until bubbly. If making for a large crowd, double recipe for a 9 x 13 casserole dish.

Miss America 2013 **Mallory Hagan** has submitted two of her Nana's recipes to Savoring the Shore in support of NJ Sandy rebuilding efforts and in honor of the pageant's return to its home in Atlantic City.

**Facing page: Margaret Gorman, Miss America 1921**
**Above: a Miss America float.**
*(Photos courtesy Miss America Organization)*

The "Show Us Your Shoes" Parade helped to create even more excitement to the festivities occurring in Atlantic City. During the annual Miss America Parade in the early 1970's, a group of spectators stationed themselves on hotel balconies overlooking the event on the boardwalk. As the contestants passed by, the overlooking spectators realized that the females were not wearing any shoes, or instead wore their bedroom slippers. After this realization, the people in the balconies began to shout "Show Us Your Shoes!" The contestants all showed off their slippers and/or bare feet to the crowd, which sparked cheers that could be heard all over the boardwalk. With this notion, a joyous tradition had begun. To this day, crowds can enjoy the excitement of the event.

Today, the Miss America Organization has continued its mission for supporting education and helping young women achieve their dreams by providing $45 million in scholarship assistance. After being in Las Vegas for nine years, the Miss America Competition will draw an even larger crowd for the return of the pageant to its original birthplace. Miss America 2013, Mallory Hagan, will accompany the 2014 National Contestants as they enter into historic Boardwalk Hall. Although a new Miss America will be crowned, Mallory will be remembered for this triumphant return to Atlantic City, and will continue to create her legacy. By being a role model to the future generation of America, Mallory has influenced and inspired others to make a difference in their community. We have been privileged to have Mallory represent the Miss America Organization as Miss America 2013.

# Green Chile Cheese Grits

*Chef Drew Araneo, Drew's Bayshore Bistro, Keyport, NJ*

Combine first 4 ingredients and bring to a simmer. Whisk in grits and reduce heat. Allow to simmer, stirring often until tender – about 20 minutes. Remove from heat and stir in cheeses.

**Chef Drew Araneo** is the chef/owner of Drew's Bayshore Bistro in Keyport, NJ. He has been named to Best Chefs America 2013 and has defeated Chef Bobby Flay in a Throwdown making Chef Drew's signature dish, VooDoo Shrimp.

2 cups chicken stock (or water)
1 Poblano chile (small dice)
Salt and pepper ("to taste"--we use about 1 Tbsp.)
1 cup grits
2 cups cheddar-jack cheese
1/4 cup Parmesan

# Fool Proof Potato Pancakes

*Jessica Mariconda*

Peel and shred potatoes (better if you use a cheese grater, but you can also use a blender or food processor if that is the consistency you like). In a bowl, mix the potatoes, eggs, and pinch of salt (to your liking). Then slowly add flour to the mixture (a little at a time) until you get the consistency of a pancake mix. Voila!  Pour into preheated frying pan with melted butter (or olive oil depending on your preference) and fry up some potato pancakes!

3 lbs. potatoes
2 eggs
Salt
Flour

# Grilled Asparagus

*John Larkin*

Preheat grill to 400 degrees F.*

Wash asparagus and remove tough ends.

Brush or spray with olive oil and sprinkle with salt and pepper.

Grill 4 minutes on first side until slightly charred.

Turn and grill second side for four minutes.

*May also be cooked on stove in frying pan over medium heat.*

Serves 4

One bunch very thin fresh asparagus
1 to 2 tsp. olive oil, spray or brush on
1/2 tsp. sea salt
1/4 tsp. freshly ground pepper

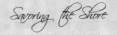
*Savoring the Shore*

# Grilled Corn on the Cob with Chipotle-Lime Butter

*Wegmans Food Markets, Trent O'Drain, New Jersey Division Executive Chef*

4 ears corn, shucked
1 Tbsp. Wegmans Basting Oil
Salt and pepper
Wegmans Chipotle Lime Finishing Butter

Preheat grill on HIGH 10 min. Coat clean grill grate lightly with vegetable oil. Drizzle corn with basting oil, season to taste with salt and pepper. Reduce heat to MED. Grill 5-8 min., turning frequently, until tender. Transfer to serving platter, top with butter.

*(Photo courtesy of Wegmans)*

# Roast Poblano - Creamed Jersey Corn

*Chef Drew Araneo, Drew's Bayshore Bistro, Keyport, NJ*

2 Tbsp. unsalted butter
4 oz. Tasso ham (small dice)
1/2 cup onion (diced)
2 Poblano chiles (roasted, peeled & diced)
6 ears Jersey corn (cut off of cob)
1 Jersey tomato (peeled, seeded & chopped)
Salt & pepper to taste
Optional – 2 Tbsp. all-purpose flour
1 cup heavy cream

In sauté pan melt butter, and add tasso ham. When ham begins to render, add onions & chiles. When onion becomes translucent, add corn. Continue to cook until corn begins to cook through. Stir in tomato, and if using flour, sprinkle over corn before adding cream. Stir in cream, season with salt & pepper, and cook until corn begins to thicken.

**Chef Drew Araneo** is the chef/owner of Drew's Bayshore Bistro in Keyport, NJ. He has been named to Best Chefs America 2013 and has defeated Chef Bobby Flay in a Throwdown making Chef Drew's signature dish, VooDoo Shrimp.

# Baked or Grilled Onions

*John Larkin with a tip of the hat to Barbara and Scott*

One small to medium onion per person
1/2 Tbsp. butter per onion
One slice of American cheese per onion (we like Land O'Lakes brand for this recipe)
Salt and pepper

For each onion: with butter, lightly grease a piece of foil large enough to loosely enclose one onion. Cut the bottom and top off each onion and remove the onion skin. Place bottom-down on foil and sprinkle with salt and pepper. Lay a slice of American cheese over the top. Loosely wrap the edges of the foil together at the top to form a packet around the onion. Bake in a 350 degree F oven for 45 - 60 minutes (depending on the size of the onion), or place on the grate of a heated grill on medium heat for about 45 – 60 minutes until the onion is softened and the cheese has melted.

Several onions at a time may be baked side by side in a greased casserole dish at 400 degrees F for about one hour or until softened and the cheese is melted. Cover with foil during the first 45 minutes then remove to brown the cheese if desired.

DAKTRONICS

> INA GARTEN
> ANNE BURRELL
> JOE BASTIANICH

*The Main Dish*

*Savoring the Shore*

# Chef Justin's Signature Crab Cakes

*Chef Justin Antiorio, Hell's Kitchen Season 10*

1/2 cup mayonnaise
2 tsp. Dijon mustard
1 red bell pepper, diced
1/2 white onion, diced
1 jalapeño pepper, diced
1 large egg
1/4 tsp. Old Bay seasoning
1 lemon (juiced and peel grated)
1 Tbsp. hot sauce
(brand of your choice)
1/4 tsp. sweet paprika
3 scallions, green parts only,
thinly sliced
1/2 bunch of parsley
1 pound lump crabmeat,
picked over for shell
3/4 cup finely ground hard pretzels
(from 1/2 lb. pretzels)
2 Tbsp. unsalted butter
1/2 cup all-purpose flour
2 Tbsp. vegetable oil

*This is the Signature Dish that Chef Justin made on Season 10 of Hell's Kitchen on the FOX Network. It is a crab cake recipe that will delight all of your senses for any occasion of your choosing. You can use this recipe to make entree portion crab cakes or 2 oz. appetizer portions.*

Sauté the peppers, onions and scallions in a pan in one tablespoon of vegetable oil until soft. Remove from pan and refrigerate the veggie mixture to cool so that you do not add hot vegetables to cold crab meat.

In a bowl, whisk the mayonnaise with the egg, mustard, Old Bay seasoning, paprika, vegetable mixture, lemon, and herbs. Fold in the crabmeat and 1/2 cup of the pretzels. Refrigerate the crab mixture for 1 hour, until the pretzels are moist.

Preheat the oven to 400 degrees F. Form the crab mixture into patties. Try using an ice cream scoop or mold to make sure each patty is consistent. Roll the cakes in a little all-purpose flour and the remaining ground pretzel to lock in the flavor and assure great consistency.

In an ovenproof nonstick skillet, melt the butter in the remaining vegetable oil. Add the crab cakes and cook over moderately high heat until browned on the bottom, about three minutes. Turn the crab cakes and transfer the skillet to the oven. Bake the crab cakes for about seven minutes, until they are heated through.

## Chef Justin's Crab Cake Sauce

*"For a flavorful sauce, I usually combine mayonnaise, mustard, couple dashes of hot sauce and a teaspoon of Old Bay." – Chef Justin*

**Chef Justin** was born in Long Branch and has frequented the shore his whole life. "So the rebuilding of the beaches and the shore means everything to me," he says.

*(Photo courtesy of the
Count Basie Theatre, Red Bank, NJ)*

# It's summer time! Get a little crabby!

*by Peg DeGrassa, Editor, Town Talk Newspapers, Delco News Network, Holmes, PA*

As soon as summer arrives, one of the things I look forward to the most is crabbing. Through the years, we've owned boats, rented boats, went out on others' boats and stood on docks, but the common denominator was we were always throwing down traps or hand lines to catch blue claw crabs. And, in my book, there are few things that are more fun or more relaxing than a morning, afternoon or day of crabbing!

Although I caught my biggest crab ever in Maryland on the Chester River (named "Crabzilla" by my family and still referenced as "legendary" to this very day), most of my crabbing has been done at the Jersey shore. The cool thing about going crabbing is it's a true family or friend bonding experience. Family members and friends of all ages can enjoy the sport together and when it's all over, everyone can enjoy a communal crab feast.

Charles Lafferty shows his grandchildren (l-r) Marguerite, Eva, Charlotte, Jim, Onnie, Marilyn, Raymond and Virginia the basket of crabs they all caught in Barnegat Bay, Ship Bottom, Long Beach Island.

My first crabbing experiences were with my grandparents who lived on Long Beach Island, year-round, and crabbed in Barnegat Bay. As a kid, I'd get my own crab trap (some call it a "crab pot") to operate. I'd always get praised when I'd pull in "some beauties," so who knows, maybe it was all this positive reinforcement going on that added to my fondness for crabbing. I was taught that we couldn't keep the females or ones that weren't big or old enough, but had to toss them back. Once in a while, I'd pull up "a bonus" to shake things up, like a spider crab, puffer fish (we called them blow fish) or more than one or two "keepers" in the trap. Once, my younger brother pulled up his trap and a lobster was in it (Yes, in Barnegat Bay!). He ended up getting his picture in the local newspaper, smiling proudly as he held the trap and the lobster (an escapee from Maine?).

Russ DeGrassa, Pat Miller, Charles and Onnie Lafferty in their "crabbing boat" netting crabs from their handlines.

According to the New Jersey tourism website, "The blue crab is known to scientists as Callinectes sapidus (kal i nek' tes sap' i dus). The literal translation of this Latin name is the beautiful (calli) swimmer (nectes) that is savory (sapidus). The blue crab certainly lives up to its name with brilliant blends of olive-green, blue and red, the ability to dart swiftly through the water and a body of delicate, white meat. Of all New Jersey's marine fish and shellfish, more effort is expended in

*Savoring the Shore*

catching the blue crab than any other single species. Surveys indicate that crabbing accounts for roughly 30 percent of all marine fishing activity."

Through the years, my family learned the "good" crabbing spots, from trial and error, and return there over and over again. The local fishery fills a drywall bucket with old smelly fish bones and yucky parts left over from filleting fish or we purchase a pack of chicken necks at the supermarket to use as our bait. As the crabs nibble the bait or it stays in the traps too long and gets waterlogged and tasteless, the bait must be replaced with "fresh" stuff to keep a good lure.

**Marguerite DeGrassa, baits her crab trap, before throwing it off the boat on a family crabbing trip in New Jersey.**

We load up our boat with the traps, some string and weights for hand lines, a wooden basket, a long-handled net, a cooler with drinks and lunch and off we go for hours. We usually only head back for a bathroom emergency (the older I get, the more we have to head back) or when the basket holds enough crabs to cook.

While out on the water, we often notice other boaters who are much more "professional" than us in their crabbing methods. Some have huge lines spread out, holding trap after trap, earmarked with bobbers or plastic milk jugs, and they run back and forth in their boats pulling up their catches like they mean business. My family, on the other hand, is always happy just to be "amateur" crabbers, with a few traps and hand lines, maybe a book in hand to read while waiting for a tug on our lines, or even a catnap snooze in the sun in between trap pull-ups. If the trip isn't enjoyable or relaxing, or resembles work in any way, you can just count me out.

A few things often add a spark or two of commotion, putting a little kink in the relaxation factor of any trip. One is when someone accidentally drops a crab into the boat as they are moving it from their trap or line into the basket. Until that crab is away from your bare or flipflopped toes, relaxation is not possible. Another thing to temporarily put a dent in relaxation is when a big boat comes along and creates a lot of wake which makes you feel like your little crabbing boat is going to tip over and you are going to end up dumped into the crab-infested water. This may not scare everyone, but it always makes me hold onto the sides of the boat for dear life. I envision all those crabs pinching away at me as I capsize into the bay! Alright, call me a drama queen. I also have never been brave enough to pick up a crab by its back feelers as others have when one fell in the boat or needed to be put in the pot. I doubt if I ever will be that courageous and so I'll leave that task for the more gutsy ones on my crabbing trips.

**Cousins Marilyn Derrickson and Marguerite DeGrassa proudly show off the cooked crabs they caught earlier in the day in Barnegat Bay.**

As we fill the basket, we continually fetch wet seaweed to cover the crabs in the basket to guard them from the hot sun. Personally, I always like crabbing with hand lines, because it feels more like a sport, a challenge. Few things feel more exhilarating than feeling a tug, seeing a huge crab on your hand line and scooping it successfully with a net. And conversely, nothing feels more defeating than when you accidentally knock it off with the net or the crab lets go of the line and stops nibbling before you can net it!

When crabbing from a boat, usually you have to try a few spots until you hit upon one that's fertile and plentiful with blues. When you find the spot, this too is an exciting moment. Person after person begins to exclaim, "Got one!" or "Wow, look at the size or this one" or "Got another big one!" At this point, the crabbing basket begins to fill up quickly and everyone's mood elevates.

After a fun day out on the boat, catching some rays and some crabs, the family or a group of friends can enjoy the fresh catch. Through the years, I've seen crabs cooked in many ways, but my family usually just puts them all in a huge crab pot with some Old Bay seasoning and a little cayenne pepper to boil, spreads out some old newspapers, throws a few nutcrackers and picker utensils on the table, grabs some cold beers and starts feasting.

Eating crabs was never much fun solo. You always want others to eat crabs with you because it is definitely a social activity, with the more, the merrier!

My parents also had a place at the shore and crabbing was always a daily activity. My dad had big commercial-like traps baited off every piling of his dock so crabs were always plentiful. Pop Pop would never let his grandchildren eat crabs until they showed him they could clean and eat a crab "without wasting any." Forget ever just eating the premium white meat when my Dad was around. Everyone would have to suck the whole crab clean or hear about it! He was the one who taught us all that there was a definite method in how to eat crabs.

In just these past few weeks, the signs and advertisements are starting to appear around Delaware County and the surrounding area- one local restaurant offers a Wednesday night all-you-can-eat crab night and another offers a crab and corn feast every Saturday in the summer. I have no interest in any of them because I know the crabs will never taste as good or as fresh, as the ones I can pull out of the bay myself. It doesn't matter if you pull your crustacean catch from the waters of Delaware, Maryland or Jersey. Summer is here and the living is easy…and the Blue Claws are running. I can't wait!

Originally published June 17, 2013, Delaware County News Network, reprinted with permission.

*Savoring the Shore*

# Ocean City Crab Cakes
*Chef Dennis Littley*

1 lb. crabmeat (claw, lump or jumbo lump- your choice)
1 Tbsp. Italian parsley finely chopped
1 Tbsp. of roasted red peppers or fresh red peppers finely chopped (may be left out)
1 Tbsp. of red onions finely chopped (you may sub any type of onion you like)
1/4 cup of seasoned bread crumbs

Imperial Sauce:
1/2 cup Hellman's mayonnaise
1 large egg
1 Tbsp. sugar
1 tsp. Old Bay seasoning
1 dash of Worcestershire sauce
1 squeeze of fresh lemon juice

*"[This is one] of my favorite recipes from my restaurant days in Ocean City… I think of…the block parties we had every spring and every fall. I could never make enough…They always sold out completely long before the day was through." –Chef Dennis Littley*

Mix crabmeat, chopped parsley, onion, and peppers together. Gently mix them, do not break up the crabmeat.

In another bowl add the mayonnaise, and egg and mix together, then add the sugar, Old Bay, Worcestershire and lemon juice, mix well. This is the imperial sauce.

Add the imperial sauce to the crabmeat and mix together gently, add in the bread crumbs and work them into the mixture.

Allow this mixture to sit for about 10 minutes. The bread crumbs will soak up any extra liquid so you can easily form the crab cakes.

Divide the crabmeat mixture into 8 small or 4 large crab cakes.

If you are frying the crab cakes, lightly coat the crab cake in seasoned bread crumbs, and sauté in olive oil till golden brown on both sides. Place in a baking dish and bake at 350 degrees F for 15 minutes.

If you are broiling the crab cakes, place them directly into a baking dish with a little bit of water in the dish. Bake at 350 degrees F for 20 minutes.

*(Photo courtesy of Chef Dennis Littley)*

**Chef Dennis K. Littley** is an executive chef, culinary instructor, recipe developer and award winning food blogger and photographer (www.askchefdennis.com and Google+ food bloggers community). He was a chef for many years at Cousin's in Ocean City, NJ and this recipe was an Ocean City favorite.

# Shrimp Puttanesca

*Jodi Roman*

In a skillet, saute olive oil, anchovies, crushed red pepper and garlic over medium heat. Once anchovies dissolve completely, add in olives, capers and tomatoes. Bring to a slow boil then add in shrimp, black pepper and parsley. Reduce heat down to simmer, and cook shrimp for 7-8 minutes. Toss with pasta and serve immediately. Enjoy!

*"[This is] a recipe from my father, Joseph Meerman, Brick, NJ"—Jodi Roman*

3-4 Tbsp. olive oil
1 tin of anchovies, drained
1/2 tsp. crushed red pepper flakes
6-7 cloves of garlic, chopped
25-30 black olives, pitted and coarsely chopped
4 Tbsp. capers
28-32 oz. can of crushed tomatoes
28-32 oz. can of diced tomatoes
Fresh ground black pepper, to taste
1/2 cup fresh parsley, chopped
1-1/2 lbs. raw shrimp, shelled and de-veined
1 lb. of spaghetti or linguine

# Shrimp Scampi with Linguine

*Chef Barret Beyer, Hell's Kitchen Season 11*

Bring a large pot of salted water to a boil. Add the linguine and cook until al dente.

Melt the butter in a large skillet over medium heat. Stir in the garlic, half of the parsley, Worcestershire sauce, lemon juice and white wine. Once the mixture begins to bubble, increase the heat a little and add the shrimp and lemon zest. Cook until the shrimp turn pink and no longer transparent in the center.

Place bed of linguine on plate or in a shallow bowl and serve the shrimp scampi mixture on top. Spoon some of the scampi sauce over linguine. Sprinkle with remaining parsley and serve!!! It's That SIMPLE!!! ENJOY!

1 box linguine
3-4 Tbsp. butter
4 cloves garlic sliced thin or minced
1 Tbsp. chopped fresh parsley
1 dash Worcestershire sauce
2 lemons zested
   then halved and juiced
1/4 cup white wine
1 lb. shrimp peeled and deveined (I use size 16-20)--leave tail on and try not to use frozen shrimp

*Savoring the Shore*

# Lobster Mac and Cheese

*Kelly Ryan, The Boondocks Fishery, Red Bank, NJ*

1 box elbow macaroni
1-1/2 lb. lobster chopped and drained
2 Tbsp. butter
1 onion, diced
2 cloves garlic, minced
1-1/2 cups whole milk
1 cup Half and Half
1 stick butter
1/2 cup flour
1 lb. Gruyere, Swiss or Emmenthaler cheese
3 cups shredded sharp cheddar cheese
1 cup grated Romano cheese
Salt and pepper to taste
Cayenne pepper to taste
1 cup panko
4 Tbsp. butter, melted

Fill a large pot with lightly salted water, bring to rolling boil, stir in macaroni and return to boil and cook according to package directions, do not overcook! Drain and cool down.

Melt 2 tablespoons butter in saucepan and cook onion and garlic until cooked through, add milk and Half and Half, bring to simmer and season with salt and pepper.

Heat oven to 350 degrees F.

Melt stick of butter in saucepan over medium heat, whisk in the flour until mixture becomes paste (roux) and cook to light golden brown. Slowly add the milk mixture to roux whisking to avoid lumps. After incorporated and starting to thicken, add cheeses one at a time and melt until smooth. Add in lobster meat, macaroni, salt and pepper and cayenne pepper to taste. Pour into pan or casserole dish. Melt 4 Tbsp. butter and stir in Panko until toasted and nutty brown. Top pasta with panko mixture. Cover pan/dish with foil and heat through in 350 degree F oven. Serve warm.

# Seared Barnegat Light Scallops, English Pea & Mint Puree, Pea Tendrils and Forest Mushrooms

*Chef Anthony Bucco, The Ryland Inn in Whitehouse Station, NJ*

## Seared Scallops:

Remove the abductor muscle off the scallops. Season with sea salt. Over medium-high heat warm a sauté pan, add blended oil. Sear scallops for 3 minutes or until golden brown. Flip scallops over; remove the pan from heat, let sit for one more minute remove scallops from pan, reserve.

4 portions

1 lb. 10/20 count day boat scallops
1 Tbsp. sea salt
2 Tbsp. blended oil

## English Pea and Mint Puree:

Cut leeks into small dice and rinse dirt off. Cook down the leeks in olive oil. Let leeks cool. Meanwhile blanch the peas in the boiling water until tender. Shock in the ice bath. Blanch the mint and shock. Take the peas, mint, and leeks and put in a blender. Add some of the ice water puree until smooth. Add water as necessary, should be thick enough to coat the back of a spoon. Taste for seasoning, add salt as needed. Pass through a sieve and keep cool.

1 pint English peas out of shell
1 large leek (white only)
2 oz. mint (just leaves)
2 Tbsp. olive oil
Salt to taste

## Forest Mushrooms:

In a pre-heated sauté pan, add bruniose of shallot to blended oil, gently sweat out, and then add mushrooms. Cook mushrooms for around 8 minutes, or until they become nice and tender. Season to taste with salt and pepper. Add lemon juice. Reserve.

1 lb. assorted mushrooms (small dice)
1 shallot (cut into bruniose)
Juice of 1 lemon
Salt and pepper to taste
2 Tbsp. blended oil

## Additional Enchantments:

2 oz. pea tendrils

## To Plate:

Pool the English Pea Puree in the middle of desired plate. Top with scallops and forest mushrooms and garnish with pea tendrils. Enjoy!

---

**Chef Anthony Bucco** has been named to Best Chefs America 2013. He is executive chef of The Ryland Inn in Whitehouse Station, NJ and a resident of Monmouth County.

# Red's Lobster Pot Homemade Lobster Cakes

*Kitty Stillufsen, Red's Lobster Pot, Point Pleasant Beach, NJ*

6 small cakes

One lb. fresh lobster meat, steamed and chopped
1/4 large green bell pepper, chopped
1/4 large red bell pepper, chopped
1/2 cup fresh bread crumbs
1 egg
Salt and pepper to taste
2 dashes of Worcestershire sauce
1 tsp. Dijon mustard
1/4 cup mayonnaise
1/2 tsp. Old Bay seasoning

### Cajun Mayonnaise:

1/2 cup mayonnaise
1/2 tsp. Cajun spice or more to taste

*"Steamed fresh N.J. lobster meat (important to use NJ lobster meat for freshness), bell peppers, homemade breadcrumbs (we use our leftover Joe Leone's bread), eggs, salt , pepper, Worcestershire sauce, Dijon mustard, mayonnaise, Old Bay seasoning, ....mix together all ingredients, including bread crumbs...form into patties. When measuring ingredients try to keep the mixture on the dry side. Measure to taste. Saute in Olive Oil, and finish in the oven, or for a crispy finish in the broiler. For an added crowd pleaser- serve with Cajun mayonnaise! Yum, Yum and more YUM!"*

*—Kitty Stillufsen, Red's Lobster Pot*

We've had the privilege of enjoying Red's lobster cakes firsthand and Kitty is so right, they are delicious! When we had them at Red's they were served with rice and steamed fresh vegetables. In making our own we used the following proportions and the results were wonderful:

Preheat oven to 350 degrees F.

Combine all ingredients and form into small cakes.

Heat small amount of olive oil in pan (we used a cast iron skillet) over medium high heat then sauté the cakes on both sides just until golden brown. Transfer skillet to preheated oven and bake for 10 minutes. (If not using cast iron skillet, transfer crab cakes to cookie sheet lightly sprayed with olive oil.)

Combine mayonnaise and Cajun spice.

Serve cakes with a dollop of Cajun mayonnaise on the side.

# Lazy Lobster

*Chef Chris Brandl, Brandl, Belmar, NJ*

## Lobster:

Cook lobsters in boiling water for 10 minutes, cool in an ice bath, then de-shell the claws, knuckles, & tail meal and reserve the shells to make a lobster stock.

## Vanilla Bean Butter:

Soften butter, scrape vanilla bean pulp into butter, add honey, and salt & pepper to taste.

## Asparagus Risotto:

In a large pot on medium to high heat add oil and butter, add onions and sauté for 3-4 minutes until onions get soft, stir. Then add rice and sprigs of thyme and stir. Season with salt and pepper. Caramelize the rice for 3-4 minutes, and stir, add wine & water or stock and reduce the heat and cook for another 7-8 minutes and stir. Cool and lay out on a sheet pan the par-cooked risotto until ready to use.

In a medium to high heat large sauté pan add oil then shallots, scallions, & asparagus sauté for 2 minutes, then add 16 oz of the par-cooked risotto then add the stock, heavy cream, and cheese. Season and stir. Keep hot.

## Poaching Lobsters:

In another large sauté pan on medium heat place the cooked lobsters, asparagus tips, and vanilla bean butter, then reheat the lobsters.

## Plating Dish:

In a 4 inch ring mold place 6 oz of the asparagus risotto in it, then place the poached lobster tail, knuckle meat, & claws, and arrange the three tips of asparagus on the plate. Drizzle with 2 oz of the vanilla bean butter. Enjoy!!!

Yield 4

4 lobsters, 1-1/4 lb. each

8 oz. butter
1/2 vanilla bean cut lengthwise
1 tbsp. honey
Salt/pepper to taste

4 oz. canola oil
2 oz. butter
1/2 large white onion, diced
1 lb. Arborio rice
3 sprigs of fresh thyme
Salt/ pepper to taste
2 cups of white wine
2 cups water
1 tbsp canola oil
1 large shallot small dice
2 scallions sliced thin
12 large asparagus spears cut on the bias, save the tips blanch them and save for garnish
4 oz. water or lobster stock
4 oz. heavy cream
4 oz. grated pecorino Romano
Salt/pepper to taste

Brandl the restaurant is located in Belmar, NJ and owner/chef Chris Brandl's Lazy Lobster is a signature dish. **Chef Brandl** has been named to the Best Chefs America 2013.

*Savoring the Shore*

# Creating a happy shore memory 1,000 miles from the shore

*Kathy Caruso Stutzman, http://mamacarusocooks.blogspot.com*

My book club reads to eat. For the past eight years we have met monthly rotating between each other's homes and December is my month because it is lobster fest. Every December. In my selfish attempt to create a fond memory of the shore, now that I live in the Mid-west, I suggested the book "Lobster Chronicles" several years ago so that we could eat lobster. We read to eat, and select food themes based upon the book we are reading and "Lobster Chronicles" seemed like a great way to introduce my friends to lobster, which many of them had never experienced.

I grew up on the East Coast where eating lobster, clams, shrimp, oysters, and crab was a was just part of my experience – from Maine to Maryland I expected a special weekend meal to include some kind of fish that had been caught nearby. Hosteling on Cape Cod, camping on the beaches in Maine or escaping a hot kitchen in Baltimore and cracking crab claws on the picnic table out back, there was always fantastic food and friendship shared. Holidays included lobster, with New Year's Eve featuring a lobster salad made from leftovers, family gatherings in Maryland ensured crab feasts, and weddings often featured hog roasts with a clam bake. My fondest childhood memories are related to family, friends and food and the extra special memories added the shore to that mix.

The sea breeze, sounds of the waves, the gulls calling out, the taste and smells that lets you know that you are somewhere alive, vibrant and salty…and the sand; cold, wet, dry, hot, rough, soft, ever-present, thousands and millions of grains of sand that come together to provide a place for the waves to connect.

The shore, oh boy…do I miss the shore here in Minnesota.  So I've decided to recreate my happy shore memories, right here with my family and friends…now all I need is the food and the ambience and my book group is all in.

So here is how I made it happen – the recipe for creating a happy shore memory 1,000 miles away from the shore:

**FOOD:**  Lobster – I begin by ordering the lobster, which includes talking to the local grocery department meat department to find out when they receive deliveries of lobster and how long they will hold them (so I can select the date), Shrimp for a shrimp cocktail, Cocktail sauce, Butter, Corn on the cob, Vanilla ice cream

I have selected the shellfish which are successful here. Clams and crab are very difficult to get fresh, and even though I have tried to order steamers, I usually end up with huge clams which are only good chopped into chowder - so lobster and shrimp it is. There are no cheddar biscuits, no fork food – part of the fun in the sharing of a feast like this is formalities go out the window. I am trying to create an experience of sitting around a picnic table, with newsprint spread out on the table, paper towels act as napkins and no one cares how much Old Bay ends up on the beer bottle. The only worry is whether or not the butter will make the wine glass too slippery. Jeans are expected apparel and dish towels act as bibs.

**EQUIPMENT & SUPPLIES:**  Plastic table cloths, Bucket for shells, Claw crackers, Picking forks – like skinny fondue forks for pulling meat out of the claws, Rolls of paper towels, Dishcloths for bibs, Large platters for each individual to act as a plate, A large canning pot for cooking the lobsters, Butter warmers

Growing up by the shore, I fully expected that all kitchens have claw crackers, and crab mallets and picking forks and small sharp knives to cut through tough shells – so for those of you reading this who would also have the same expectation, make no assumptions and plan ahead, some of this equipment may be difficult to find – and while you can substitute with common items lying around the house, it will be far more enjoyable and create a closer experience to fond shore memories to have the appropriate equipment.

**AMBIENCE:**  One CD player playing sounds of the sea recordings, if you can find one that has an occasional gull calling out – that is fun, I usually pick out a few from my local library. A second CD player playing fun music that you can envision dancing on the beach to – you can't go wrong with Reggae. Serve beer from a barrel. Put a few fans around to simulate a breeze. Encourage guests to bring flip flops and wear shorts, sunglasses as headbands. A bowl of lemons, rolls of paper towels on the tables and a large serving platter for the lobster. Pictorial instructions about how to eat a lobster I splurge and turn up the heat for the night

Each of these components will help you create a new shore memory. Have fun with it, put yourself in the experience and you and your friends and family might even forget that you are miles away from the shore. Friends, family gathering around food at the shore, it just doesn't get much better than this.

---

**Mama Caruso (aka Kathy Caruso Stutzman),** http://mamacarusocooks.blogspot.com, grew up eating her way through happy shore memories from Maine to Maryland. Just thinking about the shore evokes memories of the sounds, smells and feel for her; and creating that experience for others who have never been is a wonderful and delicious challenge.

*The Main Dish*

# Pan Grilled Scallops on Mixed Field Greens with Creamy Harissa Dressing

*Mark J. Drabich, President, Metropolitan Seafood & Gourmet, Lebanon, NJ*

In a medium bowl whisk together the lemon zest, olive oil, 1/2 tsp. salt, 1/2 tsp. pepper, the smoked paprika, and cumin. Place the Scallops in the bowl and toss gently to coat well. Cover and refrigerate for 30 minutes to 1 hour.

Preheat your grill pan or cast iron skillet to medium high heat.

To make the dressing, whisk together the Lebneh, harissa, chopped mint, and lemon juice and season to taste with salt and pepper; set aside.

Remove the Scallops from the marinade and lightly brush the grill pan with olive oil. Cook the Scallops for 2 to 3 minutes per side or until just opaque when cut into. Transfer Scallops to a warm platter and tent with foil.

Next in a large bowl, toss together greens, carrot, bell pepper, red onion, and olives with a 1/2 cup of the harissa dressing until just coated.

To serve, divide the salad among four plates and top with grilled Scallops. Drizzle remaining dressing over salads and garnish with extra mint. The only problem I see with this easy weekday recipe and massage is topping it on Saturday night. Stay Hungry my friends….

*"My fondest 'Food Shore' memory is buying my Scallops from Viking Village…the Day Boat Scallops are sublime." –Mark J. Drabish*

Serves 4

1 1/2 to 2 lbs. of sea scallops with the abductor muscle removed
 – it's not surgery it's just the little strap on the side with the Scallop where it was attached to the shell
1 tsp. of finely grated lemon zest
1 Tbsp. of olive oil
Kosher salt
Fresh ground black pepper
1/2 tsp. of smoked paprika
1/2 tsp. of cumin
1 cup of Lebneh or Greek style yogurt
1 tsp. of Harissa paste
1 Tbsp. fresh chopped mint
The juice of half a lemon
 or more to taste
1-5 oz. container of organic mixed baby field greens or other light green mix
1/2 medium red onion cut into thin half-moon slices; rinsed under cold water and dried with paper towels; this is to remove some of the heavy sulfur overtones from the onion.
1 medium carrot cut into 2 inch match sticks
1/2 of a sweet red bell pepper cut into thin strips
1/4 cup quartered, pitted Kalamata olives (Metro has these)

*Savoring the Shore*

# Pistachio-Nut Crusted Sea Scallops

*Chef and Restaurateur Adele DiBiase, Pizza Vita and Vita Organics, Summit, NJ*

1/2 cup shelled pistachio nuts
16 U-10 fresh sea scallops
3 Tbsp. salted butter
1/8 cup Chablis (white wine)
1 fresh lemon – for juicing
1-1/4 cups chicken stock
Pinch of salt
Pinch of pepper

*"This elegant, yet surprisingly easy-to-make seafood dish is perfect for entertaining a crowd of two or four. The ground pistachios create a flavorful crust on tender sea scallops floating in a buttery sauce – a palette-pleasing combination." – Chef Adele DiBiase*

Grind pistachios in a food processor until fine. Set aside.

Place sea scallops on a sheet pan. Season both sides with salt and pepper. Place butter around sheet pan. Add lemon juice, white wine and chicken stock. Top each scallop with the ground pistachios. Place in a 500 degree F oven and bake until pistachios are golden brown, about 5 to 7 minutes. Remove sheet pan from oven and place pan across two stovetop burners on high heat. Cook until all liquid reduces to a glaze. Plate 4 scallops per person.

# Grilled Mussels with Curry Butter

*allrecipes.com, submitted by Betsy Belt, reprinted with permission*

3 Tbsp. butter softened
2 garlic cloves pressed or minced
1 tsp. curry powder
1/2 tsp. ground cumin
1/8 tsp. salt

2 lbs. mussels scrubbed and de-bearded
1 cup chopped red bell pepper
1/4 cup fresh parsley chopped
1 lime thinly sliced
1 lime cut in wedges

**Curry Mixture:**

Whisk together five ingredients and set aside.

**Mussels:**

Arrange four large sheets of aluminum foil on a flat surface. Divide mussels into four even portions and place one portion on each piece of foil. Dot the mussels with the curry mixture. Sprinkle the red bell pepper and parsley over the top of each portion. Top each with lime slices. Wrap foil tightly around the portions. Cook the packets on the preheated grill until the mussels have opened, 5-10 minutes.

Discard any mussels which do not open. Transfer the mussels to small bowls and garnish each with a lime wedge to serve. Bon Appetit!

# Samantha Carrie Johnson's Steamed Clams with Chorizo

Serves 2-4

3 Tbsp. olive oil
3 cloves fresh garlic, minced
3/4 cup dry white wine
1/2 cup of whole San Marzano
    tomatoes
3/4 cup of chorizo sausage sliced into
    rounds
2 lbs. of Manila clams, rinsed and
    cleaned
3 Tbsp. fresh cilantro roughly
    chopped with stem
1 jalapeno pepper sliced
Pinch of salt
1 lime cut into wedges
Crusty baguette

*"This recipe was a favorite and top seller at my restaurant Soul in Philadelphia. I have always had a love of seafood and growing up every summer in Cape May, NJ further encouraged it. I am so grateful to call the Jersey Shore my summertime home and will continue to be inspired by its beauty, history and local fruits of the sea that contribution to our diverse food culture."*
*—Samantha Carrie Johnson*

Heat oil in a pot over medium heat. Add garlic and cook for 1-2 minutes until garlic is aromatic. Add chorizo and tomato. Add wine and increase heat to medium-high until liquid is brought to a simmering boil. Add clams and cook covered for 5-7 minutes, stirring occasionally, until clams have opened. Add jalapeno, cilantro, salt and squeeze in 1 lime wedge juice. Transfer clams and broth to a large serving bowl, serving with extra lime wedges on the side and bread for dipping.

**Samantha Carrie Johnson** is an MTV MADE Coach, Miss PA USA 2007, cook, writer, and creator of Terra 2 Table.

*Savoring the Shore*

# Fried Oysters on Toast – "A Dish Fit For a King"

*Karen L. Schnitzspahn, Jersey Shore Food History, Victorian Feasts to Boardwalk Treats*

Serves two

8 fresh large, plump oysters (shucked)
1/2 cup flour
1 egg plus 1 Tbsp. milk, beaten
1/2 cup cracker crumbs
Salt & pepper (sea salt and lemon pepper are nice)
Canola oil
1 Tbsp. dried parsley and fresh sprigs of parsley for garnish
Two lemon wedges for garnish
Two slices of buttered toast (crusts trimmed) cut into quarters

*"In nineteenth century America, an 'oyster craze' was sweeping the nation and the Jersey Shore was well known for these succulent mollusks. At Red Bank and Fair Haven, a thriving shellfish industry once prospered along The North Shrewsbury River (now known as The Navesink). Most shore eateries served oysters and a variety of delicious oyster dishes were featured on their menus. In the late 1880s, Frank Clusey's, a Red Bank restaurant on West Front St., advertised this specialty in The Daily Register: 'Fried Oysters on Toast is a dish which will give excellent satisfaction to a hungry man, and even those who aren't particularly hungry will find it delicious. Nice plump oysters, fried in cracker crumbs and served smoking hot, on delicately browned toast, make a dish fit for a king.'*

*"Based upon this vintage ad, my husband, Leon, and I decided to make a slightly enhanced and updated version of this Victorian delight. First, we purchased eight plump shucked oysters from a reliable local fish market. It's so important to use seafood that is fresh and we're lucky to live near the shore. Using three separate small bowls, we dredged each oyster in flour, then dipped them into an egg wash, and rolled them in cracker crumbs. Into each bowl, we had sprinkled some salt and lemon pepper (to taste), and parsley flakes into the cracker crumbs only. In the old days, the chefs would have fried them in lard, but we used Canola oil, our favorite cooking oil. Deep fry the oysters until golden brown and drain them in paper towels.*

*"Serve on top of buttered toast points (we used multi grain bread). Garnish with a lemon wedge and some sprigs of parsley. Eat them while they're hot and enjoy their crisp and juicy flavor! Tartar sauce goes nicely with them but is not necessary. A frosty mug of light beer pairs well with this dish.*

*"Frank Clusey's even offered "a fry in a box," (an early version of fast food 'take out' for 30 cents: 'Those men who go home late will find home a very pleasant place, even at 2am, if they take home to their wives.' Clusey's was obviously a Victorian style men's saloon and such establishments were common in the late nineteenth century.*

*"Oysters were in such demand for so many years that they were over-harvested and the supply diminished. Today, efforts by environmental groups and dedicated oyster farmers are helping to re-establish oysters on the New Jersey Coast."— © Karen L. Schnitzspahn, 2013, reprinted with permission*

**Karen L. Schnitzspahn** is the author of *Jersey Shore Food History: Victorian Feasts to Boardwalk Treats* (The History Press, 2012) and other regional New Jersey history books.

# Pan-seared Wahoo with Spring Vegetable Succotash & Lemon Thyme Vinaigrette

*Jessica Lewis, Hell's Kitchen Season 11*

Using non-stick pan, add small amount of canola oil to just cover bottom of pan. Heat on high until the pan is just about to smoke, add the Wahoo fillet skin side down pressing gently on the fillet. Immediately put in oven at 400 degrees F for about 5-6 minutes. When removing from oven, skin should be crispy. Season skin side with salt.

Bring a small pot of salted water to a rolling boil. Add snap peas, when peas turn bright green, after about 1 minute, remove and place in ice bath. After cooled, remove from ice bath onto paper towel. Split peas in half length-wise.

Heat a saute pan on medium-high heat, add butter, heat until melted. First add corn and saute until lightly browned. Next add cherry tomatoes, snap peas and garlic. Saute for about 1-2 minutes, until hot and garlic is cooked through. Season with salt and pepper to taste. Take pan off heat, last add basil and chives, stir.

To make vinaigrette - combine all ingredients and whisk to create a broken vinaigrette or blend in blender to emulsify. Enjoy!

* You can substitute a similar fish, Spanish Mackeral or Mahi Mahi.

** For a twist to the succotash, add 1/4 cup hickory bacon lardons in the pan first, cook until crispy and don't use any butter.

Serves 1

6-8 oz. Wahoo* fillet (skin on)
Salt

## Succotash**:

1 cup cherry tomatoes (red and yellow)
1/2 cup corn
1/2 cup sugar-snap peas
1 Tbsp. minced garlic
1 Tbsp. fresh basil chiffonade
1 Tbsp. finely chopped chives
1 Tbsp. butter
Salt
Fresh ground pepper

## Lemon-Thyme Vinaigrette (yield approx. 2/3 cup):

1/2 cup olive oil
1/8 cup sherry vinegar
2 lemons squeezed
2 Tbsp. fresh thyme (finely chopped)
1 Tbsp. brown sugar
Salt
Pepper

(Photo credit: Jessica Lewis)

*Savoring the Shore*

# White Fish with Heirloom Cherry Tomato Salsa

*Kate Strangfeld, Icing off the Cake, www.icingoffthecake.com*

Serves 4

15 cherry heirloom tomatoes
(about a pint),
chopped into quarters
Juice of 1 lemon
2 tablespoon chopped fresh cilantro
4 tablespoons chopped red onion
Sea salt and pepper, to taste
(make sure to put enough salt in –
it really makes the flavors pop)
4-5 ounces flaky white fish per
person, like tilapia or flounder

*(Photo courtesy www.icingoffthecake.com)*

*"This fish is about as simple as it gets: simple flavors, less than 5 ingredients, and quick to cook. If you can, buy local cherry tomatoes. You'll notice a big difference in flavor."*
*– Kate Strangfeld*

Combine tomatoes, lemon, cilantro, red onion, sea salt, and pepper in a small bowl and mix well. Set aside. (This can be done up to one day in advance)

You can either grill the fish, or if you don't have access to a grill, sauté it.

If grilling, heat a grill on medium to high heat and spray with oil. If sautéing heat a small sauté pan over high heat and spray with oil. Put fish on grill or sauté pan for about 2-3 minutes, and then flip. Remove fish from pan/grill once the fish is opaque and flakes at the touch of a fork.

---

**Kate Strangfeld** is a former NJ resident who has packed a lot of food experience into a few short years. As explained on her blog, www.icingoffthecake.com, her love affair with food kicked into high gear at the Natural Gourmet Institute for Culinary Arts and Health in Manhattan from which she graduated. She recently has worked at the *Yale Rudd Center for Food Policy and Obesity* and for First Lady Michelle Obama's *Let's Move! initiative.*

# Grilled Whole Salmon with Grilled Vegetables and Tomato Vinaigrette

*Chef David Burke, David Burke Fromagerie, Rumson, NJ*

Serves 4 to 6

1 whole salmon, cleaned, about 6 pounds, scaled, gutted and cut into two filets
Salt
3 to 4 tablespoons olive oil
14 cup minced fresh parsley
1/4 cup olive oil
Juice of 1 large lemon, about 3 tablespoons
Lemon wedges

Wash salmon and pat dry all over with paper towels. Split the salmon and rub both sides with salt and olive oil. Grease grill well. Place fish on grill flesh side down; close grill lid. Cook over moderate coals for 4-6 minutes, or until just browned. Meanwhile, mix parsley, 1/2 cup olive oil, and lemon juice. Turn fish carefully. With skin side down, rub top side with oil mixture. Close lid and cook for 7-9 minutes or until fish flakes easily with a fork. Serve warm with lemon wedges.

## Grilled corn on the cob:

Peel the husk off the corn. Rub the corn with whole butter and season with salt and pepper. Place the corn on the grill for about 10 min. rotating the corn every 2 min.

## Grilled cippollini onions:

Peel the onion, cut in half horizontally and place face down on the grill making sure it's seasoned (greased) for about 2 min.

## Grilled asparagus:

Peel asparagus and blanche in salty water for 2 min. Season the asparagus with blended oil, salt and pepper and place on the frill for about 2 min. on each side.

Preheat oven to 350 degrees F. Line a baking sheet with parchment paper and set aside.

## Grilled Vegetables and Corn on the Cob:

(yields 4 servings)

4 cobs of fresh corn
2 tbsp. olive oil
4 cippolini onions
8 pieces asparagus
2 tbsp. oil oil
Salt/pepper to taste

12 plum tomatoes
Salt/pepper to taste
2-1/2 cups olive oil
12 garlic slivers
12 sprigs fresh thyme
1 cup red wine vinegar

## Tomato Vinaigrette:

Cut each tomato in half lengthwise and place the halves on the prepared baking sheet, cut side up. Season the cut sides with salt and pepper to taste. Using a pastry brushand 1/2 cup of the olive oil, lightly coat the tomatoes. Place a sliver of garlic and a sprig of thyme on each tomato. Place the baking sheet in the preheated oven and roast the tomatoes for 20 minutes or until very tender. Remove them from the oven and allow them to cool.

When cool, remove and discard the garlic slivers and thyme. Place the tomatoes in a blender. Add the vinegar and process to a smooth puree. With the motor running on low, slowly add the remaining 2 cups of olive oil. When the mixture is fully emulsified, season to taste with salt and pepper. Pour the vinaigrette into a non-reactive container and cover it. Store at room temperature until ready to serve.

**Chef David Burke** was named NJ Restaurateur of the Year in November 2012 by the NJ Restaurant Association and in the same month received the Best Chef Concierge Choice Award "celebrating the best in NYC hospitality." He has also appeared on Bravo Network's *Top Chef Masters.* Chef Burke's restaurant Fromagerie in Rumson, NJ, features seasonal and local fare *"in homage to the abundant produce and seafood of his native Garden State."*
– www.davidburke.com

# Nancy's Fish to Shore

*Lucia Harvilchuck*

Rinse fish and pat dry. Place in shallow glass baking dish. Spread thin layer of light mayonnaise on fish. Cover with saltine cracker crumbs. Bake at 325 degrees F for 20 – 25 minutes or until a fork goes through the fish with no resistance. Place under the broiler for a minute or two—watch carefully as it will brown rapidly.

*"It is as simple, sweet and fresh as all the shore!" –Lucia Harvilchuck*

Any fish, white: cod, haddock or scrod
Hellman's light mayonnaise
Saltine cracker crumbs
Salt and pepper to taste

# Salmon with Maple Glaze

*Lori Stokes, ABC TV NY Channel 7 Eyewitness News*

Preheat oven to 350 degrees F. For easy clean up line a cookie sheet with aluminum foil. Place salmon fillets on sheet and drizzle each with 2 tsp. of maple syrup and sprinkle each with 1/2 tsp. of Old Bay. Bake for 15 minutes or until fish flakes.

*We were privileged to meet Lori Stokes and other members of the Eyewitness News Team Ken Rosato, Bill Evans, Amy Freeze and Heather O'Rourke at a Table to Table Fundraiser. The organization has strong support from area chefs and facilitates getting extra prepared food to people in need in New Jersey.*

Serves 2

2 (4 oz.) salmon fillets
4 tsp. maple syrup
1 tsp. Old Bay seasoning

# Grilled Salmon & Avocado Dip

*Adapted from allrecipes.com submitted by Margie Raff*

**Avocado Dip:**

Mix together four ingredients.

**Grilled Salmon:**

Preheat grill (lightly oil grate). Rub salmon with dill and lemon pepper. Cook approximately 15 minutes, turning once. Top salmon with avocado dip.

Enjoy!

*"Happy to submit one of my family's favorite recipes"*

2 very ripe avocados – mashed
1 tsp. minced garlic
1 Tbsp. lemon juice
6 ozs. plain non-fat Greek yogurt season with salt and pepper if you choose

2 pounds salmon steaks
2 tsp. dried dill weed
2 tsp. lemon pepper

*Savoring the Shore*

# Grilled Swordfish with Tequila and Caper Sauce over Black Garlic Infused Polenta

*Chef Barret Beyer, Hell's Kitchen Season 11*

Time: 30 Min

7-8 oz. swordfish steak
5 or 6 cloves black garlic
1 oz. capers
1 shallot
1/4 oz. fresh ground pink peppercorn
4 oz. Jose Cuervo Tequila
1 lemon
1 lime
1 tomato
Handful of cilantro
1 red onion
3 scallions
Extra virgin olive oil (EVOO)
1 cup yellow cornmeal
2 cups chicken stock
Heavy cream
Kosher salt

*(Photo courtesy of Barret Beyer)*

Heat up grill to medium heat and coat swordfish with a little EVOO and lightly salt. Also put on a medium saucepot with chicken stock and bring to a boil.

While grill is heating up in a small bowl make Pico de Gallo:

combine small dice tomato (cut out the seeds), brunoise red onion, chopped cilantro, zest of 1 lemon, zest of 1 lime, scallions cut on a long bias and juice of 1 half a lime. Mix it up and set it aside.

Place swordfish on grill and let cook about 10-12 minutes.

While swordfish is cooking mash the black garlic cloves with chef knife and add to boiling chicken stock and whisk until it is mostly dissolved into liquid. Slowly add the yellow cornmeal in a steady stream while whisking consistently until polenta starts to pull away from pot (approx 15-20 min until done).

Turn fish 90 on grill replacing it on same side it has been cooking on to make cross grill marks approx. 5 minutes. After cross marks are on fish turn it over and let cook an additional 5 min then place it on a lightly greased hot plate and put in oven at approx. 375 degrees F to finish (about 5 min).

## For Tequila Caper sauce

In a sauté pan put a little EVOO, minced shallots, ground pink peppercorn with capers and let sweat approx 3 minutes over medium heat. Pull sauté pan from stove and add Jose Cuervo and return to stove to Flambé. Let the alcohol reduce until almost dry and then add about 3 oz of heavy cream and reduce until slightly thickened.

## Plating

Spoon polenta onto dish and take a spoonful of the sauce and put over polenta. Place the swordfish grill marks up on top of the polenta and then take another spoonful of sauce and place across the swordfish. Take bowl of Pico De Gallo made earlier and place garnish on top of fish.

# Bloody Mary Tomato-Poached Chicken with Celeriac Mousse

*Chef Eric LeVine, Morris Tap and Grill, Randolph, NJ*

2 lbs. boneless, skinless chicken breasts
3 cups Bloody Mary mix
1 cup chicken stock
1 red onion, roughly chopped
1 jalapeño, roughly chopped
1 tsp. olive oil
Kosher salt
White pepper

## Bloody Mary-Poached Chicken:

Clean any fat off chicken breasts and dice into 1/4-inch pieces. Sauté onion and jalapeño pieces in oil until soft about 6 minutes. Add chicken pieces and sauté until lightly browned, about 5 minutes. Add the liquids and bring temperature to 160 degrees F. Cook over medium flame for 20 minutes, until chicken pieces are cooked through. Remove chicken pieces from pot and let cool.

4 oz. celeriac root
1 tsp. prepared horseradish
1/2 cup sour cream
1/4 bunch chervil, finely chopped (reserve the rest of the bunch for garnish)
1/4 cup heavy cream
Kosher salt
White pepper

## Celeriac Mousse:

Peel the celeriac root and then grate into a mixing bowl. Add the horseradish and sour cream to the celeriac. Then add the heavy cream and whisk briskly. Season with salt and pepper. Fold the finely chopped chervil into the mousse.

## Assembly:

Place 2 oz. of poached chicken cubes into the bottom of each glass. Put the Celeriac Mousse into a piping bag with a circle tip and then pipe on top of the chicken in each glass. Garnish with chervil.

**Chef Eric LeVine** is a Food Network Chopped champion and a partner in Morris Tap and Grill in Randolph, NJ. He is the author of *Small Bites Big Flavor: Simple, Savory and Sophisticated Recipes for Entertaining.*

*(Photo courtesy of Chef Eric LeVine)*

# Chicken with Blueberry Barbecue Sauce

*Executive Chef Christine Nunn, Grange, Westwood, NJ*

*"Skin on chicken on the grill is delicious but a bit tricky. That pesky skin just sticks to the grates. I tend to cook it skin side up, on a medium heat with the grill cover closed to crisp the skin. I add the barbecue sauce during the final minute or two of cooking so that it doesn't burn. The barbecue sauce has a blue tint to it, making it a colorful addition to a patriotic cookout." – Christine Nunn*

## Chicken:

Prepare grill: if using gas grill, set to medium, if using charcoal, set up for indirect cooking. Season the chicken skin well with salt and pepper. Place the chicken pieces on the grill, skin side up. Cover the grill, checking every 10 minutes, and rotating chicken pieces to ensure even cooking. Occasionally brush the chicken with the melted butter. Cook until chicken pieces register 160 degrees on an instant read thermometer. The wings will cook fastest, the breast will take longer. Remove pieces as they are done, and reserve on a platter. When all the chicken has cooked, return it all to the grill. Coat lightly with barbecue sauce, reserving the remaining sauce to serve on the side. Let cook an additional two minutes.

## Barbecue Sauce:

Sweat garlic and onions with olive oil in heavy bottomed sauce pan. Add ketchup and all wet ingredients. Combine well. Add dry ingredients and stir. Cook for one half hour, stirring frequently. Add blueberries and cook for an additional 45 minutes, stirring frequently. Cool or serve warm. Store up to one week sealed in refrigerator.

**Chef Christine Nunn** is the executive chef of Grange in Westwood, NJ. She has been named to America's Best Chefs 2013. She is also author of *The Preppy Cookbook* which was published in August 2013.

*Did you know that blueberries were first successfully cultivated in New Jersey? This was through a collaboration between botanist Frederick Coville and benefactor Elizabeth Coleman White. Author Karen Schnitzspahn shares the story in* **Jersey Shore Food History, Victorian Feasts to Boardwalk Treats.**

Serves four

Two fryer chickens, cut up, thighs, legs, breast, and wing (or any way you choose)
2 tsp. Kosher salt
2 tsp. course ground pepper
1 Tbsp. butter, melted

2 cups ketchup
3 cups fresh blueberries
1/3 cup brown sugar
1/4 cup minced onion
2 Tbsp. olive oil
4 Tbsp. water
3 cloves garlic crushed
3 Tbsp. apple cider vinegar
2 Tbsp. tomato paste
1 Tbsp. Worcestershire sauce
1 Tbsp. soy sauce
1 tsp. dry mustard
1/2 tsp. cayenne
1 Tbsp. cumin
2 Tbsp. chili powder
1 Tbsp. butcher grind pepper

*Savoring the Shore*

# Chicken Pot Pie

*Debby Larkin*

Serves 6

One pie crust – I use the frozen crusts from the supermarket, but use any pie crust recipe you like. Be sure it doesn't have any sugar in it.

4 whole boneless, skinless chicken breasts (2 lbs.)

1 cup heavy cream

Frozen vegetables, use what you like. I usually use a box of peas and carrots, some frozen asparagus tips, and some frozen baby pearl onions, but use what you like.

5 Tbsp. unsalted butter

2 small yellow onions (8 oz.) coarsely chopped

5 Tbsp. unbleached all-purpose flour

1 cup chicken broth (low sodium, if you have it)

1/4 cup cognac or dry white wine

1 Tbsp. dried tarragon*

1-1/2 tsp. salt (kosher)

1/2 tsp. freshly ground black pepper

1 egg

1 Tbsp. water

*"I use the recipe from The Silver Palate Good Times Cookbook, but have adapted it to make it easier. I usually double the recipe because it's a great dish for a party. Or make two and freeze one for later use." –Debby Larkin*

Preheat oven to 350 degrees F. Place chicken breasts in single layer in a baking pan. Pour the heavy cream over and bake 20 to 25 minutes. Remove the chicken from the cream; reserve the cream and cooking juices. Let the chicken cool and cut into one inch pieces.

Melt the butter in a large saucepan over medium heat. Add the onions and sauté until translucent, about 5 minutes. (You can add some sliced mushrooms with the onions.) Add the flour and cook, stirring constantly, for 5 minutes. Do not let the flour brown.

Add the broth and cook, stirring constantly, till thickened. Stir in the reserved cream and cooking juices and the cognac. Cook over low heat until thick, about 5 minutes.

Stir in the tarragon, salt and pepper and simmer 1 minute. Add the chicken and vegetables and mix gently into the cream sauce. Remove from the heat.

Preheat oven to 425 degrees F. Mix the egg and water in a small bowl. Pour the chicken filling into a deep 2-quart casserole or souffle dish. I often use a lasagna pan, so everyone gets a good piece of crust. Roll out the pie crust and place on the dish. Trim the pie crust, leaving a one-inch border. Brush the edge of the dish with egg wash and press the overhanging dough onto the dish. Crimp it decoratively and brush the top with egg wash. Cut some vents in the top. You can prepare to this point the day before and refrigerate till ready to bake. Take out of the fridge a half hour or so before you bake.

Place the pie on a baking sheet and bake on the middle rack until the crust is golden, 20 to 25 minutes. Serve immediately.

* *I like tarragon, so this suits me, but feel free to add thyme or any other herb you like instead. Or just chop a bunch of fresh parsley and toss that in. I often do that, even with the tarragon.*

*Adapted from **The Silver Palate Good Times Cookbook.***

# Spring Asparagus with Chicken & Watercress

*Chef Sharon Merkel-Prudhomme, Prudhomme's Lost Cajun Kitchen, Columbia, PA*

*"A quick and simple spring meal!"* – Chef Sharon Merkel-Prudhomme

In skillet at medium heat, add oil to prevent sticking. Add cumin and poultry seasoning – adding seasoning first allows full flavor to pop! Stir rapidly for a minute.

Add chicken chunks and sauté about 4 minutes or until done. Set aside.

Add 1/4 cup water – scrape and stir to loosen drippings and seasoning.

Place all veggies into pan, sprinkle lemon zest over all veggies along with several thin lemon slices.

Turn up heat to steam – stir slightly (add optional butter). Turn veggies over several times to allow lemon and remaining seasoning to coat all.

On plate, arrange watercress or spinach. When asparagus is slightly fork-or knife-tender (never limp!) add chicken and sesame seeds, stirring to reheat. Pepper to taste.

Spoon and arrange over watercress or spinach along with drippings and enjoy!

Oil
Cumin to taste
1 - 2 tsp. poultry seasoning
5 oz. boneless skinless chicken breast cut into bite-sized pieces
1/4 cup water for steaming
6 spears fresh asparagus, ends trimmed
One handful watercress or spinach
5 – 6 cherry tomatoes, halved
Several mushrooms, sliced
One handful red onion, sliced
Zest of one lemon – thinly slice after removing zest
Butter – optional
2 Tbsp. sesame seeds
Pepper to taste

**Sharon Merkel-Prudhomme** grew up in Spring Lake Heights, NJ and has much family and many friends at the NJ shore. Chef Sharon is one of Harrisburg, PA's ABCTV27 Mid Day Gourmet Chefs. She and her husband David (Paul Prudhomme's nephew) have operated Prudhomme's Lost Cajun Kitchen for more than 21 years in Columbia, PA. The location is a known ghost haunt featured on the cover of **"Ghosts of the River Towns"** by Rick Fisher. Ghostly dinners are periodically offered and reservations are recommended.

*Savoring the Shore*

# Chicken Lil' Lil' Dom

*Chef Dominic Bossone, Squan Tavern, Manasquan, NJ*

Serves 2

2 chicken cutlets (thin)
3 Tbsp. butter (1 reserved)
8 artichoke heart quarters
Pinch chopped parsley
1/2 tsp. pepper (to taste)
1/2 tsp. salt (to taste)
Pinch oregano
1/4 cup chicken stock
2 – 3 Tbsp. white wine
Freshly cooked pasta of your choice

Add 2 Tbsp. butter to heated sauté pan. Saute 2 pieces of chicken about 3 minutes on each side or until cooked through. Drain off most of the butter. Add artichoke hearts, parsley, pepper, salt, oregano, chicken stock, white wine and the final Tbsp. of butter. Let simmer together for about 5 minutes. Serve over the pasta of your choice.

**Chef Dominic** often names his dished after family members as well as sports teams and athletes.

# Homemade Rotisserie Chicken

*John Larkin*

Serves 4 - 6

One roasting chicken approximately 5 pounds
One stick salted butter
2 Tbsp. olive oil
1/2 tsp. salt
1/2 tsp. ground pepper

Preheat grill equipped with rotisserie to 400 degrees F

Slice butter into 1 T pats and place in saucepan. Add olive oil and salt and pepper. Stir over medium heat until butter melts.

Remove neck and gizzard package and rinse out chicken cavity.

Tie legs tight to body with kitchen string.

Tie wings tight to body with kitchen string.

Thread chicken on to rotisserie and activate.

Baste for one rotation with butter mixture.

Close cover and rotate for 1 – 1-/2 hours basting every 10 minutes until internal temperature tested in thick part of thigh is 185 degrees F and juices run clear.

Remove from rotisserie to carving board and allow to sit for 5 minutes.

Cut into serving size pieces.

# Chicken with Wild Mushroom Risotto, Asparagus

*Chef Michael Thompson, Chef Michael's Café, Wall, NJ*

*"The secret to making great risotto is that you have to stand over it and stir it constantly. It is about a 25 minute commitment and it will quickly stick to the bottom of the pan if you don't pay attention. The end result of all your hard work is a wonderfully creamy dish that will still be just a touch al dente. A couple of essential tricks to making properly are to reduce the white wine au sec (almost dry) with the sweated onion, shallots and rice. The reduction really sweetens it up and loses a lot of the alcohol taste. Also make sure to add the butter and parmesan cheese when it is totally finished cooking. At the last minute, fold it in. That takes it over the top. You can add your favorite vegetable at the end so the risotto stays white. I like to add mushrooms or do it with asparagus and Meyer lemon. And another thing, don't be cheap on the cheese! Use real Parmesano Reggiano, the salt crystals in the cheese add another layer of flavor to this great dish. Make this for someone you love tonight. Bon Appétit!" –Chef Michael Thompson*

### Risotto:

In a small saucepan, bring stock to a boil and reduce the heat to a simmer. In a different medium saucepan, over medium heat add olive oil and sauté onion, shallot and leek until translucent but not browned. Add garlic and risotto, stir for one minute. Deglaze with white wine and reduce until almost dry. Turn up heat to medium high and add 1/2 cup of warm stock or water and stir with wooden spoon, scraping bottom constantly. As liquid evaporates add another cup and keep stirring and adding liquid for about 22-25 minutes. Do not stop stirring or rice will stick to the pot and burn! Risotto is done when rice is creamy and tender – but not mushy. Remove from heat, season with salt and pepper, stir in softened butter and grated cheese. Garnish with chopped chives.

### Chicken:

Heat oven to 500 degrees F. Season chicken breasts with salt and pepper. Heat ovenproof medium sauté pan until almost smoking. Add 3 Tbsp. oil and place chicken breasts skin side down and lower heat to medium. Cook skin side down until it starts to brown about 5 minutes. Flip chicken skin side up and place in oven for 15 minutes or until cooked through. Remove from oven and reserve.

### Mushroom Broth:

Take dried mushrooms and water and bring to a boil. Reduce heat and simmer for 30 minutes until reduced by 75%. Season to taste with salt and pepper. Drain and save broth. Chop mushrooms and reserve.

### Asparagus:

Peel asparagus and blanch in boiling salted water for approximately 3-1/2 minutes until tender. Remove and place in ice bath. This process "shocks" the color into the vegetable so it stays vibrant when you heat it up. Warm up in a little water, butter and salt and pepper.

### To Assemble:

In 4 large bowls, place a scoop of risotto mixed with mushrooms, top with asparagus, then chicken. Pour mushroom broth around risotto. Serve immediately.

Serves 4
1 cup risotto (Arborio rice)
4 cups chicken broth or water
1 Tbsp. olive oil
1/2 white onion, minced
2 shallots, minced
2 Tbsp. unsalted butter, softened
1 clove garlic, minced
1 leek, white part only, minced
1/2 cup Parmesano Reggiano cheese, grated
Salt and pepper
1/2 cup white wine
Chives, garnish

For the Chicken:

4 – 8 oz. chicken breasts, skin on

For the Mushroom Broth:

1 cup dried mushrooms
2 cups water

For the Asparagus:

16 pieces jumbo asparagus, peeled

*Savoring the Shore*

(Photo courtesy of Chef Michael Thompson)

**Chef Michael** is a California native who trained at the prestigious California Culinary Academy in San Francisco and subsequently with award winning Master Chef Julian Serrano of Masas in San Francisco. He moved to NJ in 2005 and has recently opened Chef Michael's Café in Wall. He says, "If you are too busy to make this dish yourself, you can always hire Chef Michael Thompson to make it for you in your home. Contact him at 732. 948. 2352 or michael@ chefmichaelthompson.com."

# Magret a la D'Artagnan

*Ariane Daguin, http://www.dartagnan.com/*

With a knife, score the skin of the magret making the squares as small as possible without cutting into the meat. Season with salt and pepper on both sides. Place in a hot skillet skin side down and reduce heat to medium. Cook for 8 minutes, while continuously draining off the rendered fat.

Flip over and cook for 4 minutes on the meat side. On a heated grill, finish cooking on the meat side for 4 minutes. Cover the magret with foil to keep warm and set aside.

Drain fat from pan, leaving 1 tablespoon of fat in pan. Sauté the shallots in the rendered duck fat until they are translucent. Add wine and reduce by half. Add demi-glace and reduce by half again. Season with salt and pepper.

Slice magret in 1/4 slices. Lay slices on warm plates in a fan pattern.

Spoon sauce over magret slices and serve with green beans and scalloped potatoes.

2 D'Artagnan Magret Duck Breasts
   (available online at
   http://www.dartagnan.com/)
1 shallot, finely chopped
1 cup Madiran or other red wine
2 tablespoons D'Artagnan Duck and
   Veal Demi-Glace
   (available online at
   http://www.dartagnan.com/)
Salt
Pepper

## Variations:

*Fruits:* at step 8, add your favorite fresh berries, grapes or chopped fruits (apples, pears, etc.)

*Herbs:* at step 8, add your favorite fresh herbs, finely chopped

*Peppercorns:* at step 8, add a few tablespoons of your favorite peppercorns

*Butter:* at step 10, whisk in 2 tablespoons of Black Truffle Butter

**Reprinted with permission of D'Artagnan**

*(Photo courtesy of D'Artagnan)*

*Savoring the Shore*

# Carmine's Meatballs and Sauce

*Carmine's Real Italian of New York and Atlantic City*

Makes about 12 meatballs and
6 cups of sauce

1-1/2 lbs. of ground beef, such as
chuck with 20% fat
1/2 pound of veal
2 large eggs beaten
1/4 cup seasoned bread crumb
3 Tbsp. chopped flat-leaf parsley
2 Tbsp. chopped fresh basil
1 Tbsp. salt
1 tsp. finely chopped garlic
1/2 tsp. freshly ground black pepper
4 slices firm white bread, crusts
removed
1 cup milk
1 cup grated Romano cheese
2 oz. and 2 teaspoons olive oil
4 oz. Spanish onion, peeled
and diced small
1 Tbsp. chopped garlic
10 cups Carmine's Marinara sauce

In a large mixing bowl, use your hands or a wooden spoon to mix together the beef, veal, and eggs. Add the bread crumbs, parsley, basil, salt, garlic, and pepper and mix it well.

Tear the bread into pieces and transfer it to a mixing bowl. Add the milk and let it sit for 5 to 7 minutes or until the milk is nearly absorbed. Add the bread to the meat and use your hands or a wooden spoon to mix well. Stir in the 1/2 cup grated cheese. Cover the bowl with plastic wrap and refrigerate it for 45 minutes to 1 hour or until the meat mixture is firm.

Use an ice cream scoop, remove chunks of meat and roll them between dampened palms into meatballs, each weighing about 3 ounces. Refrigerate the meatballs for at least 10 minutes before proceeding with the recipe.

To sauté the meatballs, heat 2 oz. of the olive oil in a large sauté pan over medium-high heat. When the pan is hot, add the meatballs and cook them for about 10 minutes, turning them gently until they are browned on all sides. Transfer them to a platter and set them aside. Drain excess grease.

In the same pan, heat the remaining 2 tsp. of olive oil over medium-high heat. Add the onion and garlic and sauté them 6-10 minutes or until they are browned.

Meanwhile, in a large pot large enough to hold the meatballs, heat the marinara sauce over the medium high heat for 6-8 minutes or until the sauce boils. Stir in the onions and garlic.

Add the browned meatballs and any accumulated juices and cook them over medium heat for about 45 minutes. Do not cover them while cooking. Add remaining 1/2 cup Romano cheese. Remove them from the heat and set them aside for about 45 minutes or until they have had ample time to mellow and the flavors of the sauce and meat intermingle. To store the meatballs, let them cool in the sauce. Transfer them to a tightly lidded storage container and refrigerate them for up to 1 week or freeze them for up to one month.

*"Carmine's Real Italian is so glad to be a part of the Shore Family. We've been in Atlantic City for almost 10 years, and we are excited to be there for many more! Use this recipe to make our famous meatballs in the comfort of your own home. You can use any type of homemade or store-bought marinara sauce; just make sure to give the meatballs time to settle for a while to ensure all the flavors come together!"*

# Ponzu Spiced Beef Short Ribs & Cucumber-Apple Salad with Meyer Lemon Citronette

*Chef Dominick Hayman*

6 oz. (cut into 2" sections) beef short ribs
1 Tbsp. Ponzu sauce (or low sodium soy sauce)
1tsp. chili powder
1/2 tsp. paprika
1/8 tsp. cinnamon
1/4 tsp. cumin
1 tsp. garlic (minced)
1/2 tsp. turmeric
1/2 tsp. kosher salt
1/4 tsp. ground black pepper
1/2 tsp. canola oil

1/2 of 1 English cucumber
1/2 of 1 (cored) Pink Lady or Golden Delicious apple
1/4 tsp garlic (minced)
Juice of 1 Meyer lemon juice
Zest of 1 Meyer lemon zest
1/3 tsp. kosher salt
1/4 tsp. agave nectar
1/4 tsp. cilantro (chopped)
1-1/2 oz. olive oil

Add all spices and ponzu to short ribs in a medium bowl and mix until surface of ribs are completely covered. Let marinate for at least 30 minutes. Heat medium saucepan over medium high and add canola oil. Once pan is hot add marinated ribs and sear for 1-1/2 minutes on each side. Remove ribs from pan and allow to rest for 3 minutes. Serve hot with cucumber-apple salad.

Add minced garlic, lemon zest, and salt to a medium metal mixing bowl and using the back side of a metal tablespoon grind and press the contents. This will release the oils of the zest and garlic. After grinding for 2 minutes add the juice of one Meyer lemon and stir, then gradually add olive oil while stirring to create an emulsion. Finish by stirring in agave nectar until dissolved. Set citronette aside and begin to shred cucumber using a large grater. Next remove core from apple and cut into thin slices; thinly julienne these slices. Add cucumber and apple to citronette and toss together with chopped cilantro. Serve at room temperature or chilled.

**Chef Dominick Hayman** and this recipe took first place in the "Top Chef" competition at the Black Culinary Expo 2013 in Brooklyn, NY.

# Chile-Rubbed Skirt Steak with Heirloom Tomato Salad

*Chef Ivy Stark, Dos Caminos*

Lightly toast the cumin seeds in a dry skillet until their aroma is released. Place in a blender. Add the jalapenos, garlic, black pepper, salt and lime juice and puree until the cumin seeds are finely ground; then add the cilantro, olive and salt and puree until smooth.

Brush the meat with the chile rub. Heat the grill to very hot, cook the steaks until seared on both sides 3-4 minutes. Slice the steak thinly on the bias.

Place the steak on a serving plate with fresh tomato and red onion slices, and a few cilantro leaves. Drizzle tomato, onion and cilantro leaves with sherry vinegar, extra virgin olive oil, sea salt and freshly cracked black pepper. Crumble queso fresco over the tomatoes. Serve with warm tortillas on the side.

---

**Chef Ivy Stark** is Executive Chef of Dos Caminos, New York, and is ranked among New York's top chefs. Dos Caminos is also located at Harrah's Atlantic City Resort.

1/4 cup cumin seeds
4 jalapeno chiles, stemmed, cut in half and seeded
3 garlic cloves, peeled
1 Tbsp. freshly cracked black pepper
1/4 cup freshly squeezed lime juice
1 bunches cilantro, stems and leaves (reserve a few leaves for garnish)
1/2 cups olive oil
1 tsp. salt
2 lbs. skirt steak
2 ripe heirloom or red tomatoes, sliced
1 medium red onion, thinly sliced
2 oz. queso fresco, crumbled
1 Tbsp. aged sherry vinegar
1 Tbsp. extra virgin olive oil
Sea salt and freshly cracked black pepper
Tortillas for serving

# Grandma's Sauce

*Jessica Mariconda*

Run tomatoes through a food mill until smooth. Add 1 tsp. salt and halved garlic cloves. Bring to a simmer over low heat, do not boil. Partially cover and let simmer for 30 minutes. Meanwhile heat olive oil, 2 cloves of garlic, sliced onion. Add meat and brown. Remove and discard the onion and garlic. Add the tomato paste to the pan with the meat and oil, cook 1 minute. Add one can of water (using tomato paste can) and stir until well combined. Add frying pan contents to the tomato sauce pot. Add cheese, partially cover, and simmer over very low heat for 2-3 hours stirring occasionally.

*"Before anything, the secret to good Italian gravy is to add a little bit of sugar. For the recipe above, remember it is a basic gravy, meaning that you can add anything you want to it to make it your own (i.e. oregano, crushed red pepper if you like a little kick, whatever you like!). But remember the sugar (it's always the secret ingredient that most Italians don't like to tell you) – tomatoes are naturally acidic, you could add about 1/2 teaspoon of sugar to the recipe and it cuts the acidity. Also the flavor of the gravy will depend on the sausage you use. Some sausages are very salty so be careful with that. If you are using a salty sausage, then cut back on any salt." – Jessica Mariconda*

1 can of Italian style tomatoes
1 small can of tomato paste
Italian sausage (or pork), optional
Chuck steak, optional
1 tsp. salt
4 cloves of garlic
1 onion, sliced
Olive oil
Salt
Parmesan cheese

# Braised Boneless Short Ribs of Beef with Crispy Frizzled Onions

*Branches Catering, West Long Branch, NJ*

2 lbs. boneless short ribs
1-1/2 gallons of beef broth
1/3 cup of olive oil
Salt and pepper to season
1 medium onion
6 stalks of celery
3 carrots
2 endives
2 cloves of garlic

4 cups of frying oil
Salt and pepper for seasoning
1 large onion
Flour for dredging

### Short Ribs:

In a stockpot, heat olive oil over medium heat. Season short ribs with salt and pepper and add to pot and sear on all sides. Add the remaining of the ingredients and season with salt and pepper. Stir. Add beef broth and simmer over medium heat for 45 minutes to 1 hour until broth has reduced. Top with frizzled onions to serve.

### Crispy Frizzled Onions:

In a separate stockpot, heat olive oil over medium high heat to 375°. Thinly slice onion and season liberally with salt and pepper. Dredge in flower and shake off excess. Deep fry onions until golden and crisp, about two minutes. Onions will turn one shade darker once out of the oil.

Branches Catering's Jersey Shore location has been a "Hospitality Landmark" since its founding as Joseph's Restaurant in February 2002 at the former address of Squire's Pub in West Long Branch, NJ. Branches completely renovated the 14,000 S.F. facility and constructed a manicured waterfall garden in 2005. The name Branches comes from a stately magnolia tree that graces the front of the building.

# Stuffed Cabbage

*Jessica Mariconda*

1 head of cabbage
2 cups cooked rice
2 lbs. of chopped meat
Touch of salt
Touch of pepper
Touch of milk (optional)
1 can of tomatoes
(or a bowl of the homemade gravy – red sauce – is better!)

Core and boil whole head of cabbage in water with salt. Drain and pull each leaf off the head of cabbage.

Cook 1 cup of raw rice (will make 2 cups of cooked rice).

In a bowl, combine 2 lbs. of raw chopped meat, 2 cups of cooked rice, touch of salt and pepper (to your taste) and a touch of milk to bind it all together. Mix it all together like you are making a meatloaf.

Fan out one cabbage leaf and put a meatball size of the meat into the center of the cabbage. Fold in the sides of the cabbage and roll cabbage leaf closed.

In a large gravy pot line the bottom of the pot with a thin layer of gravy (red sauce). Place a row of the rolled stuffed cabbage in the bottom of the pot. Layer a small amount of gravy on top of the bottom layer of cabbage. Repeat the layer of stuffed cabbage and gravy until you fill the pot.

Simmer for 1 hour covered. To check that the meat in the whole pot is cooked all the way through, cut open one of the stuffed cabbage on the top, if the meat is cooked on the top layer, then it will be cooked on the bottom!

# Dan's Mom's Famous Savory Meat Pie

*Chef Dan Alpaugh*

## Crust :

(yields one 9 to 10" double crust pie):

Combine flour and salt in mixing bowl. Using your hands, work butter into flour and salt mixture to incorporate until mixture forms small pea-size balls. Add ice water 2 Tbsp. at a time. Work dough until you are able to pinch cough without being tacky. Shape dough to a 1" thick disk. Wrap in plastic wrap. Refrigerate one hour or up to one day ahead. Roll into 13-14" round 1/8" thick. Transfer to a 10" pie plate. Roll second dough to a 12" round 1/8" thick. Refrigerate 15 minutes.

2-1/2 cups all-purpose flour
1-1/4 tsp. kosher salt
2-1/2 sticks unsalted butter, cut into 1/2" pieces
5 Tbsp. ice water

## Filling:

Preheat oven to 350 degree F. On stove in pan, heat oil. Season beef with salt and pepper then sear in hot oil. Remove beef and add onions to pan. Saute to soften then add carrots and celery. Deglaze with wine, then add tomatoes and tomato juice, rosemary, bay leaves, wine and beef stock. Reduce heat to simmer, add beef cubes and salt and pepper. Simmer, covered, 1-1/2 hours or until tender. Thicken juice with cornstarch dissolved in water. Stir to incorporate. Add filling to pie shell. Top with top crust. Bake in a 350 degree F oven for 25 minutes or until top is light brown.

1/2 cup each of the following vegetables: carrots, celery, onion, potatoes, peas
4 large bay leaves
1 cup beef stock
1/4 cup tomato juice
2 Tbsp. crushed tomato
1/4 tsp. fresh rosemary
Sea salt, black pepper to taste (TT)
1 lb. beef brisket cut into 1" cubes
2 Tbsp. red wine
1 tsp. cornstarch
1 tsp. water
2 Tbsp. olive oil

*"It always seems we had this around St. Paddy's Day, a rich comfort food, to be shared with friends and family. Being a CIA grad and chef of a very popular South Jersey Italian Import Company, I know this dish would make Mom proud. We've sold it in the stores [Joe Leone's], now you can enjoy it in your home. Enjoy!" –Chef Dan Alpaugh*

*Savoring the Shore*

# Pork Loin Roulade with Mushroom, Spinach and Jack Daniels Cream Sauce and Smashed Roasted Garlic Potato

*Chef Barret Beyer, Hell's Kitchen Season 11*

8 oz. pork loin
Handful of fresh spinach
6 shitake mushrooms
6 oyster mushrooms
1 shallot
5 red potatoes
12 garlic cloves
4 oz. Jack Daniels
8 oz. heavy cream
Extra virgin olive oil (EVOO)
1 Tbsp. fresh ground black peppercorn
Kosher salt
2 oz. pine nuts
5 oz. grated Parmesan
Flour

Preheat oven to 400 degrees F.

Put 5 garlic cloves in metal container with oil and roast approx. 30-35 minutes or until slightly brown.

Bring medium sauce pot of salted water to a boil and put quartered red potatoes in with skin on and let cook approx. 25 minutes or until fork tender.

Start at bottom of pork loin approx 1" from the bottom and slice until the loin is one flat piece. Cover with plastic wrap and pound out until it is about 1/2" thick and lightly salt and pepper. Sear both sides on grill and set aside.

In a sauté pan add a little EVOO and place mushroom mixture into pan and sauté until tender. Add spinach and pine nuts toss a few times to just wilt spinach and remove from heat. Place mixture across the loin evenly and sprinkle with Grated Parmesan Cheese. Roll the loin up and place it seam side down onto a lightly greased hot plate or baking tray and place in oven for about 25-30 minutes.

In a sauté pan put a little EVOO and minced garlic and sauté for about 3 minutes. Add the fresh ground black peppercorn. Pull from heat and add Jack Daniels and then return to heat to Flambé until almost dry.

Add about 3 oz. of heavy cream and let reduce while sprinkling a little parmesan cheese in sauce to thicken. Put in the halved cherry tomatoes at the very end before plating.

Take out the roasted garlic from oven. Drain water from red potato and add garlic, heavy cream salt and pepper and smash the potato with skin on.

Slice the shallot very thin, flour and place in fryer for approx. 1 minute then set aside for garnish

Pull the pork loin from oven when cooked all the way through and place on cutting board. Scoop smashed potatoes onto plate then slice the pork loin approx. 1"-2" thick. Fan out laying it aside the potato. Spoon the sauce over the bottom half of the loin and then top it off with your fried shallots and serve.

# Asian BBQ Ribs

*Wegmans Food Markets, Trent O'Drain, New Jersey Division Executive Chef*

Preheat grill on HIGH 10 min. Preheat oven to 350 degrees F. Coat cleaned grill grate lightly with vegetable oil Season both sides of ribs with seasoning. Sear on grill 3-4 min. per side; do not cook through. Transfer ribs to braising pan. Whisk BBQ sauce and beer together in bowl until well-blended; pour over ribs in pan. Cover pan; place in oven. Bake 2-1/2-3 hours. Carefully remove lid; bake 10 min. Remove ribs from pan; skim fat from top of liquid. Add pan with liquid to stovetop; bring to a simmer. Reduce liquid on medium, 12-15 min until glaze consistency is reached. Transfer ribs to serving platter; spoon reduced glaze over all.

1 rack (about 3 lbs.) center cut pork spare ribs, halved
1 Tbsp. Wegmans Orange Ginger Seasoning Shak'r
1 bottle (20 oz) Wegmans Asian-Style Hot BBQ Sauce
12 oz. lager beer

## Option(s):

Garnish with a drizzle of sesame oil and chopped onions.

*It was 1916 when brothers Walter and Jack Wegman began to sell produce from a pushcart wagon in the streets of Rochester, New York. This was the humble beginning of Wegmans Food Markets, still family-owned today, but now with 81 stores in six states. By the early 90s, Wegmans had expanded its reach beyond its home in New York State with a store in Erie, Pennsylvania and a plan to open more PA stores and eventually enter the New Jersey market.*

*Wegmans believed they could bring a unique shopping experience to New Jersey consumers, one that didn't already exist, combining incredible customer service, the best ingredients, help with meals, restaurant-quality prepared foods, and consistent low prices.*

*Selective in choosing sites, Wegmans scoured the state for ideal locations. The first store opened in 1999 in Princeton. By 2006, with the opening of the Cherry Hill store, there were seven Wegmans Food Markets in New Jersey. In 2001 and 2004, stores opened in Manalapan and Ocean.*

*(Photo courtesy of Wegmans)*

*Savoring the Shore*

# Carolina BBQ Braised Pork Butt

*Chef Drew Araneo, Drew's Bayshore Bistro, Keyport, NJ*

1 boneless pork butt (about 6-8 lbs.) cut into 3" x 3" pieces (or any manageable size)

Marinade:

1/2 cup bourbon
1/2 cup molasses
1 cup cider vinegar
2 cups white wine
1 Tbsp. Liquid Smoke
6 cloves garlic (smashed)
4 bay leaves
4 sprigs thyme
1 small can chipotle chile (6 oz.)

Combine all marinade ingredients and pour over pork. Allow pork to marinate at least overnight, but 24 hours would be great, turning every few hours. Remove pork from marinade, and pat dry. Season pork with salt & pepper and sear off in large saute pan until browned on all sides. Return pork to marinade after searing. Add water to bring liquid up to top of pork. Place in 325° F oven, and braise for 2-1/2 to 3 hours.

Remove from oven, and allow pork to cool in liquid.

To finish, remove pork from cooled liquid. Remove any fat from surface of liquid, strain, and place over high heat to reduce. When reduced pour liquid back over pork, and place in oven to heat pork through.

**Chef Drew Araneo** is the chef/owner of Drew's Bayshore Bistro in Keyport, NJ. He has been named to Best Chefs America 2013 and has defeated Chef Bobby Flay in a Throwdown making his signature dish, VooDoo Shrimp.

# Stuffed Pork Chops

*Sarah Pritchard, PritchardPhotography@Live.com*

Serves 4

4 pork chops 1" thick
Olive oil for browning
1/2 cup pesto sauce (purchased green pesto is a good choice)
1/2 cup plain croutons, slightly crushed
1/4 cup chopped softened sun-dried tomatoes or roasted red peppers

Preheat oven to 325 degrees F.

Combine pesto, croutons and tomatoes or red peppers. Set aside.

Slice a pocket in each pork chop. Heat about 2 Tbsp. olive oil in skillet and brown both sides of pork chops (add more olive oil if needed). Remove pork chops from pan and cool slightly. Stuff each chop with pesto mixture. Bake in the preheated oven for 45 minutes.

*"Though I am not a 'Jersey Girl,' I have now lived here in NJ longer than I have lived anywhere as an adult. While I traveled much of the globe, I was introduced to flavors and ingredients that were delicious! I wish I had been more adventurous with my palate – but here is an easy meat entrée with some 'unordinary' flavors mixed together that you will love!" – Sarah Pritchard, PritchardPhotography@Live.com*

# Pork and Squash Pasta

*Chef Brian Goodman*

Peel and cube squash, be sure to remove seeds and pulp. Place pot of salted water on stove, bring to boil.

In large sauté pan, place 3/4 lb. butter and add cubed squash. Once squash begins to soften, add sage, nutmeg and cinnamon. Let butter and squash brown, once squash begins to fall apart add heavy cream. Puree in blender and set aside

In a medium sauté pan, place a tablespoon of butter, and add pork and bacon. Allow to render out until crispy and golden brown. Add sage to pan, let crisp. In the meantime drop garganelle in boiling pot of water, let cook until al dente.

Take squash puree and fold in 2 tbsp. to pork. Add brodo or pork stock to squash and pork, taste and season. Once garganelle is cooked, combine with sauce, let sauce and noodle get to know each other over medium heat for a minute. Toss thoroughly and eat!

*The Greenhouse Tavern is an award-winning restaurant in downtown Cleveland, Ohio (Bon Appetit Top Ten Best New Restaurants 2009, Food and Wine Best New Chefs 2010). It also has a definite NJ shore connection through Chef Brian Goodman.*

1 small kabocha squash
   (substitute Hubbard if
   unable to find)
1 lb. butter
2 sprigs sage
1 pinch nutmeg
1 Tbsp. kosher salt
1 stick cinnamon
2 cups heavy cream
4 Tbsp. braised pork
1 Tbsp. diced bacon
1 cup brodo or pork stock
1 package garganelle pasta

**"Chef Brian Goodman's** formal training began at Rutgers University, graduating third in his class and earning a Cordon Blanc Award. Goodman then worked professionally in New Jersey kitchens where he was introduced to sustainable practices and the farm to table movement…

Goodman earned a spot with Charlie Palmer & Jonathon Sawyer at Kitchen 22, where he became Executive Chef in 2004. After a brief time at The Union Square Café he reconnected with Chef Sawyer to open Parea, working under Iron Chef Michael Symon. He remained at Parea until moving to Cleveland in 2008 to open The Greenhouse Tavern, where is now Chef/ Partner. In 2011, he defeated 20 local chefs in the Maker's Mark Chef Jam competition at the Rock and Roll Hall of Fame. In 2012 Goodman appeared as a featured sous chef in Kitchen Stadium on Iron Chef America.

Most recently he was named one of Restaurant & Hospitality Magazine's 9 to watch in 2012.

Goodman's style of cooking is heavily influenced by the Mediterranean….He currently resides in Cleveland, Ohio but still talks like he's from the Jersey Shore." –www.thegreenhousetavern.com

Chef Goodman says he still loves all things Jersey like "pork roll, Great Adventure and the Beach."

thegreenhouse
*tavern*

*Savoring the Shore*

# Black Thai
*Sean O'Leary*

2 cups of cooked black rice
2 13.5 oz. cans coconut milk
1 16 oz. can black beans
4 cloves of garlic, smashed and diced
Large handful of fresh string beans, trimmed
2 Portobello mushrooms, sliced thin
Large handful of mini peppers, sliced thin
2 stalks Bok Choy, chopped
1/2 bunch scallions, chopped
1/2 inch of ginger, diced
1 Tbsp. olive oil
4 Tbsp. sesame oil
1 Tbsp. curry powder
1/4 Tbsp. curry paste
3 Tbsp. soy sauce
1 Tbsp. turmeric
2 Tbsp. hot sauce (Siracha)
Salt and pepper
2 Tbsp. Braggs Liquid Aminos
1 Tbsp. lemon zest
2 Tbsp. peanut butter

Heat olive oil and 1/2 of sesame oil (2 Tbsp.) in large sauté pan. Add string beans, mushrooms, peppers, scallions, pinch of salt. Cook about 7 minutes over medium/high heat. Add Bok Choy, liquid amino and continue cooking for 5 minutes.

Move cooked veggies to large mixing bowl. Mix in cooked rice and lemon zest.

In original large sauté pan, add remaining sesame oil (2 Tbsp.), then garlic and ginger. Saute 2 minutes over medium/high heat. Add remaining ingredients: coconut milk, black beans, soy sauce, peanut butter, turmeric, curry powder and curry paste, hot sauce. Bring to a boil, then simmer for 5 minutes.

Stir sauce into mixing bowl and let stand for 5 minutes. Enjoy!

We first learned about **Sean O'Leary** from an article by *Lauren Payne* in the June 2013 issue of ***New Jersey Monthly Magazine***. He continued to work two shifts as a first responder with New Jersey Natural Gas for months after Superstorm Sandy, even as his own home in Point Pleasant had been heavily damaged by the storm. An "avid cook", his kitchen was the first space that he restored.

# Spinach Stuffed Shells with Béchamel Sauce

*Lorrie DiStefano*

Preheat oven to 375 degrees F.

Boil water for shells and cook until about 1 minute LESS than directions on box for al dente. Pour cold water over shells to stop the cooking and drain.

Chop onion to a fine chop and sauté about 5 minutes (until clear).

Squeeze out the spinach until it is as dry as possible then add to the onion in the pan. Stir occasionally. Continue cooking about 5 minutes.

Meanwhile, cut mozzarella into very small pieces and add them to the ricotta in a large bowl. Add 1 beaten egg and about a handful of grated cheese. Add the spinach and onion. Mix well.

In saucepan, melt the stick of butter. Add cornstarch and mix well so as not to have lumps form. When completely incorporated with butter, immediately add the milk stirring until it begins to thicken like pudding. At this point add in two beaten eggs. Continue stirring. Turn off heat. Mix in grated cheese (about a cup or more to taste).

Fill the cooked shells and put in 9x13 casserole dish. Cover with the sauce then sprinkle with a little grated cheese. Cover and cook at 375 degrees F for 30 minutes or until center of shells is hot.

1 box large pasta shells
1 (10 oz. box) frozen chopped
  spinach, thawed
1 large part-skim mozzarella
1 (32 oz.) part-skim ricotta
Grated Parmesan or Romano cheese
1 large onion minced
4 cups milk
1 stick unsalted butter
6 Tbsp. cornstarch
3 large eggs
Olive oil

# Welsh Rarebit

*Cheryl Larkin*

*"Karen Schnitzspahn, author of **Jersey Shore Food History Victorian Feasts to Boardwalk Treats**, shares a menu from 1912 that includes Welsh Rarebit – which was also a dish served as a Sunday night supper by a grandmotherly friend of my family's when we were growing up. We've re-created it and my family loves it. It's fast and flavorful."– Cheryl Larkin*

In a large saucepan or Dutch oven, make a white sauce. Start by melting 1/4 lb. unsalted butter in the pan over medium heat. When melted, add the flour one Tbsp. at a time, stirring to combine. Watch carefully and stir often. When combined, add one cup milk, stirring as ingredients combine and thicken. Grate onion over mixture and add Worcestershire sauce, Tabasco, dry mustard, and lager, beer or ale stirring to combine. Reduce heat to low and stir occasionally. May be served on slices of toast as prepared below or in a bowl with thick chunks of bread for dipping.

Arrange bread slices on a baking sheet. Rub with garlic and spread lightly with unsalted butter. Place under broiler on high for several minutes until golden brown. To serve, place toast on plate and spoon hot sauce over the top. Garnish with chopped chives if desired.

Serves 4

1/4 lb. unsalted butter plus 1 – 2 Tbsp.
  additional to spread on bread
3 Tbsp. all-purpose flour
1 cup milk
1/2 small onion, grated
1 tsp. Worcestershire sauce
2 drops/shakes Tabasco
1 tsp. dry mustard
1/2 cup lager, beer or ale
1 lb. extra sharp cheddar cheese
1 clove garlic, sliced in half
Good quality bread
Chopped chives for garnish (optional)

*Savoring the Shore*

# Yogurt with Spinach, Oregano, and Garlic Borani esfenaj

*Louisa Shafia, author, The New Persian Kitchen*

Makes 2 1/2 cups

2 Tbsp. olive oil
1/2 lb. spinach
1 Tbsp. dried oregano
1 clove garlic, minced
2 cups Greek-style yogurt
2 Tbsp. lemon juice
Salt and pepper

*"Nothing ties a Persian meal together like creamy and tangy yogurt. Yogurt is usually served as a condiment with classic dishes like lean and juicy kebab, fragrant stew, and fluffy white rice. Sometimes yogurt is served with just a sprinkling of fresh dill or dried mint, but often it's mixed with a vegetable to give it color and texture. This delicate yogurt condiment has few ingredients but holds a big, rich flavor. It's best to cut off any thick, fibrous spinach stems before cooking. Like many Persian dishes, this yogurt tastes even better after chilling overnight in the refrigerator." – Louisa Shafia*

Heat a skillet over medium heat and add the oil, followed by the spinach. Sprinkle the oregano and garlic over the spinach. Toss gently, and cook until the spinach is very tender, and most of the water has cooked out, about 10 minutes. Let the spinach cool to room temperature, then chop it finely. Fold the spinach into the yogurt, along with the lemon juice. Season with salt and pepper, and serve.

**Louisa Shafia** is the author of **The New Persian Kitchen.** In a review, Martha Rose Shulman of The New York Times writes of the book, "Every once in a while I pick up a cookbook and want to cook everything in it, which was the case with this one."

# Awesome Chicken Marinade

*Laura Currie*

1/4 cup of Dijon mustard
1/2 cup of white vinegar
2 Tbsp. minced fresh onion
1-2 cloves of garlic, crushed and minced
1/4 tsp. dry or 1 tsp. fresh rosemary, crushed

Mix all of the above together in a bowl or heavy duty gallon sized plastic bag. Add chicken and coat with mixture. Marinate for 45 minutes to several hours and grill. Covers up to 2-3 lbs. of chicken. Can be multiplied for larger amounts.

# Brandy Sauce

*Andrea DeRosa*

1 stick butter
2 Tbsp. Worcestershire sauce
2 Tbsp. mustard
1/2 cup chili sauce
1/2 cup brown sugar
1/4 cup brandy
(Harvey's Bristol Cream)

Melt butter and add all ingredients in saucepan. Cook on low, do not boil. Can be made ahead and refrigerated for up to a week. Reheat to serve.

*Hint: I most always double this recipe. It is excellent on pork, beef and more. Enjoy!*

*The Main Dish*

Sweets

# Cherry Clafoutis
*Chef Michel Richard*

Serves 6

18 ounces of fresh cherries, pitted, or
16 ounces of frozen unsweetened
dark cherries, thawed and drained
1 Tbsp. plus 1/2 cup sugar
1 tsp. cornstarch
1/2 cup all-purpose flour
1/3 cup sliced, toasted almonds
4 eggs
1/2 tsp. salt
1 cup whole milk
1 tsp. vanilla extract

Preheat oven to 300 degrees F. Butter six 7 ounce crème brulee dishes or a shallow oval custard dish. Toss the cherries with 1 Tbsp. of the sugar and the cornstarch. Next arrange the cherries in the bottom of the prepared dishes. Place the toasted almonds and flour together in a food processor and process until the almonds are finely chopped. Whisk the eggs, salt and 1/2 cup of sugar in a bowl. Then whisk in the flour mixture. Add the milk and vanilla; whisk until a smooth batter forms. Then pour the batter over the cherries, leaving a little bit of the cherry exposed. Bake in the center rack for 25-30 minutes until golden brown on the top. Remove from the oven and allow to cool for a few minutes. Then dust each dish with a little powdered sugar. Serve warm.

**Chef Michel Richard** is a James Beard award winning chef, restaurateur and artist who has also cooked with Julia Child. Chef Richard is opening the pastry shop and café Pomme Palais in New York in the fall of 2013. It is located in the NY Palace Hotel at 30 E. 51st Street.

*(All photos and artwork courtesy of Chef Michel Richard)*

# Lady Fingers

*Miss America 2013 Mallory Hagan*

Preheat oven to 350°F. Mix dough thoroughly and roll into finger shapes about 3 inches long. Bake for 30 minutes. Roll in powdered sugar while warm.

*Miss America 2013 Mallory Hagan has submitted two of her Nana's recipes to Savoring the Shore in support of NJ Sandy rebuilding efforts and in honor of the pageant's return to its home in Atlantic City.*

*(Photo courtesy of the Miss America Organization)*

2 sticks margarine
1 Tsp. vanilla flavoring
2 cups cake flour
1-1/2 cups chopped pecans
5 Tbsp. powdered sugar
(Save remainder of box of powdered sugar for rolling cookies)

# Governor's Squares

*Cathy Craven*

Preheat oven to 350 degrees F.

Line cookie sheet with whole crackers in single layer. Melt sugar and butter. Boil 2 minutes stirring constantly. Immediately pour over graham crackers. Sprinkle nuts over all. Bake 10 minutes at 350 degree F. Cool completely and cut into squares with pizza cutter.

12 graham crackers
1 cup dark brown sugar
1 cup butter
1 cup finely chopped pecans or walnuts

*Savoring the Shore*

# St. Joseph's Day Pastry

*Chef Joe Introne, Joe Leone's, Point Pleasant Beach and Sea Girt, NJ*

8 oz. water
Pinch of salt
3oz. shortening
1.5 oz cake flour.
4 oz. bread flour
8 oz. eggs
Pinch of baking powder
.25 oz. vanilla extract
2 oz. milk

## Cruller Pastry Recipe

Add water, salt and shortening into a saucepot and bring the mixture to a boil.

Sift together both flours and then whisk the flour into the boiling mixture, until totally incorporated. Then remove the mixture from the heat and pour it into a stand mixer.

Whip the mixture on a medium speed then add the eggs one at a time to incorporate.

Then add the milk and baking powder and whip continuously for 3 more minutes.

Then place the mixture into a piping bag and pipe using a large star tip, pipe the mixture into circles with hollow center (donut-shaped).

Lastly fry the dough in a pot or deep fryer at 400 degrees F until crullers are golden brown.

48 oz. milk
12.5 oz. sugar
2 cups milk (cold)
3 oz. cornstarch
6 1/2 oz. eggs
1 oz. vanilla extract

## Vanilla Custard Recipe

In a mixing bowl whisk together 2 cups of milk, the eggs, vanilla extract and the cornstarch.

Place the 48 oz. of milk and the sugar in a pot and bring it to a boil then whisk in the egg mixture from #1. Continue to whisk vigorously until the mixture thickens.

When mixture reaches pudding-like consistency, take off of the heat, strain through a strainer and refrigerate until cold.

## Assembling the Pastries:

Once the crullers and the pastry cream are fully cooled, slice the crullers horizontally.

Next place the custard in a piping bag and pipe the custard around the inside center of the bottom half of the cruller.

Then place the top half of the cruller on the custard-filled bottom.

Dust the pastry with powdered sugar and top it with a cherry.

*"Established in June of 1997 as a single building bakery & specialty store, Joe Leone's has grown into an award winning specialty food retailer with two locations offering an expansive array of imported Italian groceries, homemade breads, fresh mozzarella, gift baskets, and traditional & adapted Italian prepared dishes, paired with a full-service off-premise catering operation serving Monmouth & Ocean Counties." –www.joeleones.com*

*(Photo courtesy of Joe Leone's)*

# Saltine Toffee Cookies

*Betsy Belt*

Preheat oven to 400 degrees F.

Line jelly roll pan with saltine crackers in a single layer.

In a saucepan combine the sugar and the butter. Bring to a boil and boil for 3 minutes. Immediately pour over saltines and spread to cover crackers completely.

Bake at 400 degrees F for 5 to 6 minutes. Remove from oven and sprinkle chocolate chips over the top. Let sit for 5 minutes.

Spread melted chocolate and top with chopped nuts. Cool completely and cut or break into pieces.

4 oz. saltine crackers (this works out to be one sleeve)
1 cup butter
1 cup dark brown sugar
2 cups semi sweet chocolate chips
3/4 cup chopped pecans

# "Oreo" Stuffed Chocolate Chip Cookie Brownies

*Melissa Maria Festa - Mrs. Highlands United States 2013*

Preheat oven to 350 degrees.

You may use any pan size you like but for this recipe I used a 9 x 13 inch pan. Spray the pan with cooking spray. Spread the cookie dough evenly covering the entire pan. Add a layer of "Oreo" cookies to cover the layer of cookie dough. In a medium-size bowl stir in the vegetable oil, water, eggs and the brownie mix until blended. Then pour the mix over the "Oreos" covering the entire layer. Add another layer of "Oreo" cookies on top of the mix then pour the rest of the mix on top covering the Oreos.

Bake for approx. 45 minutes or until firm to the touch in the middle of the pan.

Let it cool for approximately 15-20 minutes.

*Mrs. Highland United States 2013 Melissa Maria Festa reigned with a platform of "Restore the Shore, Hope for Highlands" in response to Hurricane Sandy.*

"Oreos" are also special to NJ. According to the web site About.com 20th Century History, they were first introduced in 1912 by NJ-based NABISCO (National Biscuit Company). More than 362 million "Oreos" were sold from 1912-1999, making them the most popular cookie of the century. Today, in addition to supermarkets everywhere, "Oreos" may also be found on NJ boardwalks as Fried "Oreos."

Serves up to 16

1 package "Oreo" cookies (any type you prefer)
1 large roll of chocolate chip cookie dough (any type of cookie dough)
1 package of brownie mix
2 eggs
1/4 cup water
1/3 cup vegetable oil

*Savoring the Shore*

# Peanut Butter Chocolate Chip Cookies

*Anna Linn Currie*

2 cups flour (I have used whole wheat pastry or unbleached all-purpose)
1 tsp. baking soda
3/4 tsp. fine grain sea salt
1 cup natural peanut butter (the kind that separates and you have to mix together)
1 cup maple syrup
1/3 cup extra virgin olive oil
1-1/2 tsp. vanilla
3/4 - 1 cup chocolate chips

Mix flour, baking soda, and salt in a bowl. In a separate bowl mix the peanut butter, maple syrup, olive oil, and vanilla. Then add the flour mixture and stir until just combined. Add the chocolate chips and stir a couple more times.

Place somewhat flattened rounded tablespoons about 1 inch apart from each other on a baking sheet.

Bake for about 10 minutes or until the cookies look set and matte instead of glossy.

**Note:** *if baking on a glass pan the cookies will take about 2 times as long to cook.*

*Adapted from the food blog 101 Cookbooks*

# Sugar Cookies

*Christine Kennette, CK's Cookies*

1 cup sugar
1 stick butter
2 cups flour
1/4 tsp. salt
1/2 tsp. baking powder
1 large egg
1 tsp. vanilla

**Cookies:**

Preheat oven to 325 degrees F.

Using electric mixer, cream butter and sugar until fluffy. Add eggs and beat on low until combined. Then add flour, salt and baking powder and beat on low until combined. Finally add vanilla and beat until combined. Wrap dough in plastic and refrigerate for 30 minutes.

On lightly floured surface roll out dough to 1/8" thickness with rolling pin lightly dusted with flour. Cut dough with cookie cutter(s) and carefully transfer with spatula to cookie sheet. Bake for 8-10 minutes until lightly golden, not brown. Cool.

4 level tsp. powdered egg white reconstituted in 4 Tbsp. warm water
Juice of one lemon (approx. 2-1/2 Tbsp.)
3-1/2 cups confectioner's sugar
Optional food coloring as desired

**Frosting:**

Beat egg whites until fluffy but not dry, have peaks but are still shiny. Add sugar and continue to beat. Add lemon juice and beat for one minute. If too thick, add a little water. If too thin and runny add more sugar. Add food coloring as desired.

*Find CK's Cookies on Facebook at https://www.facebook.com/pages/CKs-Cookies/155774217823538*

# Mystery Cake

*Bette Jacobson*

### Cake:

Put all ingredients in bowl and mix well. Bake at 325 degrees F for 60 minutes for loaf cake. Adjust time for varied size pans. After the cake is cool frost with cream cheese frosting.

### Cream Cheese Frosting:

Beat all ingredients together until creamy. Refrigerate leftovers.

*"One of my best friend's moms made this when I was about 12 and I loved it and was intrigued by the soup!"*
*–Bette Jacobson*

1 cup sugar
1 cup tomato soup
1-1/2 cups flour
1/2 cup chopped nuts
1 tsp. cloves
1 tsp. baking soda
1 cup raisins
1 tsp. cinnamon
1 tsp. nutmeg
2 Tbsp. butter

Frosting:

1 package (8 oz.) cream cheese
1-1/2 cups powdered sugar
1 egg white

# Peanut Butter Cup Ice Cream Cake

*Kate Morgan Jackson, Framed Cooks, www.framedcooks.com*

Line a loaf pan with either plastic wrap or parchment paper. Use enough so that it hangs over the side by a few inches. Press half of ice cream into the bottom of the pan. Scatter half the peanut butter cups over the ice cream. Press the remaining ice cream on top, and scatter the remaining peanut butter cups on top along with the pretzels. Press down slightly so they adhere to the ice cream. Put the loaf pan into the back of your freezer (where it is coldest) and freeze for at least 6 hours until it is firm (and up to overnight).

Remove from the freezer and using the overhang of the wrap or paper carefully lift it out of the pan. Peel the wrap off and transfer to a serving platter. Drizzle with chocolate sauce. Cut into slices and serve at once.

3 pints of your favorite vanilla ice cream, softened
30 small chocolate peanut butter cups, chopped
1 cup mini pretzel twists, broken into pieces
Chocolate sauce, heated as needed for drizzling

**Kate Morgan Jackson** is a food writer for *The Morris County Daily Record* which you can find online at www.northjersey.com/food_dining. Her food blog is *www.framedcooks.com* where she notes, "I really do love to cook, and I really do cook every day...but the catch is, it has to be ready in 30 minutes or less, from walk in the kitchen to sitting on the table ready to be eaten. (Except for weekends when I am perfectly happy to spend all day in the kitchen.)"

*Savoring the Shore*

# Beet Chocolate Cake

*Debbie Peterson, 180 Health www.180healthonline.com*

Serves 12-16

Heat oven to 325°F. Grease two 9" cake pans or one large 13x 9 rectangular pan.

4 oz. unsweetened chocolate

Melt very slowly over low heat or in double boiler. Stir often. Watch carefully as the chocolate can easily burn if you don't keep stirring. Set aside to cool.

Dry Ingredients:

Whisk dry ingredients together.

2 cups coconut palm sugar
2 cups flour (suggestions:
1 cup spelt, 1 cup oat flours OR
gluten free flour)*
1/2 tsp. salt
2 tsp. baking powder
1 tsp. baking soda

*Gluten free option, vegetarian*

photo credit: Rebecca Gagnon
www.icakewalk.blogspot.com

Wet Ingredients:

Mix wet ingredients

4 organic free-range eggs
1/4 cup coconut oil, melted
3 cups shredded beets
(about three small beets)

Blend thoroughly with eggs and oil. Combine flour mixture with chocolate mixture, alternating with the shredded beets.

Pour into pans. Bake until fork can be removed from center cleanly 40-50 minutes.

*"My kids say that they hate beets, and to be honest, I'm not a big fan either, despite my knowing the amazing benefits packed into that bright red root. So, I have to find ways to get these benefits and enjoy them too. This is one of those ways – and everyone loves it."*
*– Debbie Peterson*

# Chocolate Zucchini Cake

*Laura Currie*

2-1/2 cups of flour
(I use whole wheat pastry flour)
1/2 cup cocoa
2-1/2 tsp. baking soda
1 tsp. salt
1 tsp. cinnamon
1 tsp. baking powder
2 tsp. vanilla
1/2 cup butter softened
(or margarine if you prefer)
2 cups sugar
3 eggs
2 cups coarsely grated zucchini
1/2 cup semi-sweet chocolate chips
1/2 cup milk

Preheat oven to 350 degrees F. Combine flour, cocoa, baking powder, baking soda, salt, and cinnamon; set aside. With a rotary mixer beat together butter and sugar until smooth. Add eggs one at a time, beating well after each addition. Stir in vanilla, chocolate chips and zucchini with a spoon. Alternately stir dry ingredients and milk into the zucchini mixture. Pour into a greased and floured Bundt pan. Bake at 350 degrees F for 50 minutes to 1 hour.

# Mom's Card Game Cake

*Submitted by Lisa Rudy Matalon in honor of her mother Liela Rudy
and in memory of her grandmother Rena Franco*

Mix filling in small bowl; set aside.

Grease Bundt pan and pre heat oven to 350 degrees F.

## Make batter:

Beat butter and sugar. Add eggs, sour cream, vanilla; mix. Add flour, sugar baking powder, baking soda, salt; mix. Put half the batter in the greased bundt pan; sprinkle with half of the filling mixture. Repeat with the remainder of batter and filling mixture. Bake at 350 degrees F for roughly 45 minutes. Let cool.

*an equal amount of apricot nectar may be substituted for the sour cream to bring down the fat*

**Liela Rudy (left) and Rena Franco**

Batter:

1 stick butter
1 cup sugar
2 eggs
1 cup sour cream*
1 tsp. vanilla
2 cup flour
1 tsp. baking soda
1 tsp. baking powder
1/2 tsp. salt

Filling:

1 package good quality chocolate chips
1/2 cup chopped walnuts (pecans work too!)
2 tsp. cinnamon
1/4 cup sugar

*Savoring the Shore*

**Sixth birthday party, grandparents' back yard, Bradley Beach, 1968**

"In the 60's and 70's we summered in Bradley Beach because my grandparents, Nat & Rena Franco, owned property there. I have sweet memories of feeding the ducks at Fletcher Lake, going to the Penny Arcade at night after our baths, buying candy from the little shop in the basement of the Brinley Hotel, French fries in that little foil bag from the Sand Bar.... But my best memories are of my Grandma Rena's cooking!

Each summer we would pick whatever produce her garden yielded and pickle or can them (that was actually the genesis for the Artisan Jam company my sister and I eventually created, Crave Jams). Grandma Rena also made a lot of traditional Middle Eastern delicacies (our family has roots in Allepo, Syria), but my fave was always her all American Sour Cream Bundt Cake! When we were little we called it Mom's Card Game Cake, because that was mainly when we got to have it. Mom or Grandma would invite the ladies over for Bridge or Mahjongg and put out a full spread and this cake was ALWAYS dessert! My mom still has a copy of the original recipe in my Grandma Rena's handwriting (who passed away in the early 1990s, healthy, in her mid-90s!) and I still have the original handwritten copy MY mom gave me when I got married three decades ago!"
– Lisa Rudy Matalon

**Teenagers at Bradley Beach, 1969**

*(All photos courtesy of Lisa Rudy Matalon.)*

# Confections of a Rock$tar's "Tequila Sunrise"

*Confections of a Rock$tar, Asbury Park, NJ*

## Cupcakes:

Preheat the oven to 325 degrees F. Sift the dry ingredients: flour, baking powder and salt in a small bowl, set aside. Zest and juice the limes, set aside. Mix the butter and sugar on medium speed for about 5 minutes until fluffy. Add the eggs and beat until combined. Add the lime zest and juice, vanilla and tequila. Mix until combined. Add half of the dry ingredients and 1/4 cup buttermilk, mix on low speed. Add the remaining dry ingredients and 1/4 cup buttermilk, mix briefly on low speed to fully incorporate.

Line a cupcake pan with cupcake liners; scoop batter evenly into each. Sprinkle with salt before baking.

Bake 20-25 minutes or until toothpick comes out clean. Remove from oven and and brush the tops of the cupcakes with tequila. Cool completely before frosting.

## Frosting:

Whip the butter and slowly add the confectioner's sugar until fully mixed. Add lime juice, tequila and salt, beat until fluffy. Top with a lime slice garnish and clear sanding sugar (gives the appearance of salt).

Makes 12 cupcakes

Cupcakes:

1-1/2 cups flour
1-1/2 tsp. baking powder
1/8 tsp. salt
1/2 cup butter, softened
1 cup sugar
2 eggs
2 large limes (or 3 medium)
4 Tbsp. tequila (white/clear)
1/4 tsp. pure clear vanilla extract
1/2 cup buttermilk

Frosting:

1 cup butter, softened
3 cups confectioner's sugar
1 Tbsp. lime juice
2 Tbsp. tequila (white/clear)
1/8 tsp. salt
Clear/white sanding sugar

*"Confections of a Rock$tar is the Jersey Shore's newest bake shop, located at 550 Cookman Avenue, in the heart of the revitalized downtown Asbury Park. Recently chosen as "Editor's Pick" by CBSLocal.com for New Jersey's Best Cupcakes, the shop offers delectable cupcakes, cookies, scones, custom cakes, gluten-free French macarons and so much more. All products are baked fresh daily and have musically-themed names, such as "Tequila Sunrise" featured here. For more information, visit us on Facebook or www.CoaRock.com."*

*(Photo courtesy Confections of a Rock$tar)*

# Chocolate Profiteroles

*Diane Manion-Loil*

Makes 20 to 24 puffs,
serve 2-3 per person

1/2 cup whole milk
1/2 cup water
8 Tbsp. (1 stick) butter, diced
1/4 tsp. sugar
1 level tsp. coarse sea salt (or 1 scant
tsp. fine salt)
1 cup flour
4 eggs (approx. 9 oz.)
3 Tbsp. of powdered sugar

### Choux Puffs:

Preheat oven to 425 degrees F.

In a heavy-bottom saucepan, over low heat, combine the milk, water, butter, sugar and salt. Bring just to a boil. Turn off the heat and add the flour while stirring continuously until flour is incorporated and dough comes away from side of pan. Quickly add the eggs one at a time and stir to incorporate. Stir until smooth. Batter will be thick and sticky. Line two large baking sheets with parchment paper. Place tablespoon size/dollop of batter widely spaced on pan. Bake one sheet at a time. Can sprinkle with powdered sugar prior to baking. Should end up with 20 to 24.

Bake 12 minutes at 425 degrees F then turn down heat to 400 degrees F and bake 10 – 12 minutes more. Should be puffed and lightly browned. Cool on wire rack. Cut each puff horizontally. Fill with ice cream and top with chocolate sauce (recipe below) or may be frozen for later use.

3/4 cup milk
7 oz. dark chocolate (Valrohona if
available)
1-2 tsp. rum or cognac, optional

### Dark Chocolate Sauce:

Gently heat milk in top of double boiler. Mix in chocolate. Stir until completely combined. Sauce will be thick and glossy. Add alcohol and stir to combine. You can make sauce ahead of time and reheat before serving.

# Pumpkin Pie with a Kick

*Sarah Pritchard, PritchardPhotography@live.com*

2 uncooked pie shells—your own or
ready-made (don't use graham
cracker, they're too sweet)
1 – 29 oz. can unflavored pumpkin
1 cup brown sugar
1 cup sugar
Dash of salt
1/2 tsp. ground clove
1/2 cup brandy
4 eggs
3 tsp. ground ginger
3 tsp. cinnamon
1 tsp. nutmeg
1-3/4 cup Half and Half

Combine pumpkin, sugars, salt and spices into on bowl. Slightly beat eggs separately then add to first bowl. Add cream and brandy and mix well by hand. Pour equally into the two pie shells. Bake 10 minutes at 450 degrees F then reduce heat to 350 degree F and bake an additional 40-50 minutes. Use toothpick to check for doneness. Best served with real whipped cream.

# Terry's Fresh Blueberry* Pie

*Cheryl Larkin*

Heat 3/4 cup sugar and 1/2 cup water in saucepan until sugar dissolves. Add 1 cup berries. Stir mixture and crush berries with the back of the spoon as you bring to a boil. Reduce heat and boil slowly, stirring, for 5 minutes. Add cornstarch dissolved in water and stir until liquid thickens, then continue to stir for one minute more. Cool slightly and fold in remaining berries. Pour into baked pie shell and chill for at least two hours. Top with whipped cream.

8" baked pie shell
3/4 cup sugar
1/2 cup water
1 qt. fresh blueberries
2 Tbsp. cornstarch dissolved in
    2 Tbsp. water
Whipped cream

*Great made with peaches or
  strawberries also!*

# Peaches and Cream Tart

*Diane Manion-Loil*

### For crust:

Crumble macaroons (2 cups) in large bowl. Stir together macaroon crumbs, pecans and margarine. Press mixture onto bottom and up sides of 11" tart pan and removable bottom. Bake at 350 degrees F until golden brown 15 – 18 minutes. Cool on wire rack.

### Filling:

Chill medium mixing bowl and beaters of electric mixer. In chilled bowl beat whipping cream on medium speed until soft peaks form and set aside.

In small mixer bowl beat cream cheese and sugar on medium speed until fluffy. Add rum or juice, vanilla, and almond extract. Beat until smooth. Gently fold in whipped cream. Turn mixture into crust. Cover and chill 2 – 4 hours.

Make glaze by combining preserves and honey in saucepan. Cool slightly.

### Assembly:

Toss peaches in lemon juice. Arrange peaches and raspberries over filling. Brush glaze lightly over fruit. Refrigerate leftovers.

9 soft coconut macaroons
    (1/2 of a 13-3/4 oz. package)
1 cup (4 oz.) ground pecans
3 Tbsp. margarine or butter melted

1/2 cup whipping cream
1 8 oz. package cream cheese
    softened
1/3 cup sugar
2 tsp. dark rum or orange juice
1 tsp. vanilla
1/4 tsp. almond extract
2 – 4 medium peaches
    (1-1/2 to3 cups), peeled and pitted
    and thinly sliced
2 Tbsp. lemon juice
1/4 cup apricot preserves
1/2 cup fresh raspberries
2 tsp. honey

*Savoring the Shore*

# Peach & Berry Cobbler

*Chef Drew Araneo, Drew's Bayshore Bistro, Keyport, NJ*

8 large Jersey peaches (peeled and sliced)
1 pint berries (blackberries if available)
3/4 cups sugar
1/2 cup flour (or more)

2 cups flour
4 Tbsp. sugar
2 tsp. baking powder
1/4 tsp. salt
1/2 cup buttermilk
1/2 cup heavy cream
1 stick unsalted butter

**Filling:**

Combine fruit and sugar and allow to macerate for at least an hour. Stir flour over fruit to help bind moisture.

**Topping:**

Combine dry ingredients in mixer. Add liquid at low speed until dough begins to form then add butter leaving visible lumps. Chill dough before using.

**Assembly:**

Place fruit in baking dish, and top with pieces of cobbler dough. Sprinkle sugar over dough, and place in 350 degree F oven. Bake until topping puffs up and turns golden (30 - 45 minutes).

**Chef Drew Araneo** is the chef/owner of Drew's Bayshore Bistro in Keyport, NJ. He has been named to Best Chefs America 2013 and has defeated Chef Bobby Flay in a Throwdown making his signature dish, VooDoo Shrimp.

# Apple Crisp

*Sarah Caldwell*

4 large apples peeled and thinly sliced
1 Tbsp. lemon juice
1 cup butter (unsalted) softened
1-1/2 cups brown sugar
1-1/2 cups quick oats
1 cup flour
2 tsp. cinnamon
Optional ice cream or whipped cream

Preheat oven to 350 degrees F. Toss apple slices in lemon juice and evenly distribute in a 13"x9" pan

Combine softened butter and dry ingredients in a bowl creating a crumbly mixture and distribute over the sliced apples until desired amount of crumb is achieved. Bake at 350 degrees F for 45 minutes or until apples are bubbling and the topping is slightly brown. Serve with ice cream or whipped cream if desired

**Fun variation:**

Serve Apple Crisp with butter pecan ice cream in individual parfait glasses.

*(Photo by Ken Caldwell)*

# Berry Mascarpone Tart

*Chef and Restaurateur Adele DiBiase, Pizza Vita and Vita Organics, Summit, NJ*

### Pie Crust:

In a food processor pulse the butter and flour until combined. Add salt and cold water. Pulse until dough comes together. Roll out dough and form it into a fluted tart pan. Chill for 30 minutes. Blind bake by covering the pie crust in aluminum foil and weighing it down with dried peas, lentils or beans. Insert into a 350 degree F oven for 30 minutes until golden.

1-1/4 cups of all-purpose flour
1/4 tsp. salt
1/2 cup chilled unsalted butter
4 Tbsp. ice water

### Topping:

In a small sauce pan add balsamic, sugar, corn starch. Whisk together. Bring to a boil. Reduce by half until mixture becomes thick and syrupy. Let cool

2 pints blueberries
2 pints raspberries
1/2 cup balsamic vinegar
1/2 cup sugar

### Filling:

Add all chilled ingredients into a mixer with a whisk attachment. Whip until fluffy peaks form. Watch carefully as the mascarpone can separate. Add filling to the cooled crust and top with fresh berries. Using a fork drizzle the balsamic reduction over the tart. Serve cool.

16 oz. mascarpone cheese
1 quart heavy cream
1 cup sugar
4 Tbsp. vanilla extract
1 pinch salt

*"This sweet and tart creation is a fluffy and creamy confection made with mascarpone cheese and topped with fresh berries and Balsamic syrup. It's perfect for entertaining a crowd.... 'Eat responsibly and save room for dessert.'" – Chef Adele DiBiase*

# Grilled Peaches

*Kate Kurelja*

Pre-heat your grill to moderate heat. Halve and pit each peach, and lay cut side up on a cutting board. Sprinkle 1/2 teaspoon of raw sugar over each peach half. Let the peaches sit while the grill is heating. When the grill is hot, place the peaches cut side down on the grates. Grill the peaches for about 5 minutes or until the sugar caramelizes and the fruit softens.

Serves 4

4 ripe, but firm Jersey peaches
4 tsp. raw sugar
Butterscotch or caramel sauce
1 cup heavy cream

Remove the peach halves from the grill. Place two halves on each plate to let cool. Meanwhile pour the heavy cream into a bowl and beat on high speed until medium peaks form. Scoop a dollop of whipped cream onto each serving of peaches. Finally drizzle each plate with your favorite butterscotch or caramel sauce. Enjoy!

*Savoring the Shore*

# Bread Pudding

*Chef Dennis K. Littley, www.askchefdennis.com*

One loaf of potato bread, cut into cubes, more if you need it, the bread should mound high above your casserole dish.
4 cups of whole milk
3 large eggs
2 cups of sugar
2 Tbsp. pure vanilla
1/3 cup raisins (optional)
1/2 stick of butter melted
1 cup of Half and Half or heavy cream

Cream Cheese Frosting:

1/2 lb. butter, softened
1 lb. cream cheese softened (not whipped)
1 cup of 10x sugar (more if you like it sweeter)
2 tsp. of pure vanilla extract

The first thing you want to do is find a proper baking dish or casserole to bake this in, around a 13x9 inch pan.

In your mixer or a large container, mix the milk, eggs, sugar, and vanilla together, making sure all the eggs are beaten in to the milk and all the sugar has been incorporated. When it is well mixed, pour this mixture over the cut bread, mixing it well so that all of the bread has absorbed some of the milk. Let it sit for at least 15 minutes (overnight in the fridge is even better). Before baking, pour the cup of half and half over the bread, this will enhance the flavor of the pudding, do not mix it in, just let it seep into the bread.

Drizzle the melted butter over the entire pan letting some of the butter's richness touch as much of the top of the mixture that it can. Cover the pudding with cling plastic wrap and then cover it with foil.

Bake for one hour at 350 degrees F, then uncover and continue to bake for 15 minutes more or until center is fully set. (If the butter has pooled in any area, spread it around before the final 15 minutes. This will help get it golden brown.)

## Cream Cheese Frosting:

Whip the butter and cream cheese with your mixer at high speed to get some air into it. With your mixer turned down to low add your 10x sugar and turn up the speed gradually. Add the vanilla and mix well

Now if you would like to do a little something else to drive your friends into a frenzy, add a little liquor or brandy to the frosting, not a lot just a tablespoon or two. Then when you put this cream cheese frosting on the warm bread pudding, the aromatics will be incredible!

**Chef Dennis K. Littley** is an executive chef, culinary instructor, recipe developer and award winning food blogger and photographer (*www.askchefdennis.com* and Google+ food bloggers community). He was a chef for many years at Cousin's in Ocean City, NJ and this recipe was an Ocean City favorite.

# Peanut Butter Mousse and Chocolate Mousse with Hazelnut Sauce

*Chef Eric LeVine, Morris Tap and Grill, Randolph, NJ*

## Peanut Butter Mousse:

Cream the cream cheese with powdered sugar in the bowl of a stand mixer with balloon whisk attachment. Add the milk and peanut butter. In a separate mixing bowl, whip the cream and vanilla. Once they are incorporated, fold into the peanut butter mixture.

3 oz. cream cheese
1 cup powdered sugar
1/4 cup milk
3/4 cup peanut butter
2 cups heavy cream
1 Tbsp. vanilla

## Chocolate Mousse:

Whip the cream to soft peaks, then refrigerate.

Combine the chocolate, butter, and espresso in the top of a double boiler over hot, but not simmering, water, stirring frequently until smooth. Remove from the heat and let cool until the chocolate is just slightly warmer than body temperature. To test, dab some chocolate on your bottom lip. It should feel warm. If it is too cool, the mixture will seize when the other ingredients are added.

Once the melted chocolate has cooled slightly, whip the egg whites in a medium bowl until they are foamy and beginning to hold a shape. Sprinkle in the sugar and beat until soft peaks form.

When the chocolate has reached the proper temperature, stir in the yolks. Gently stir in about one-third of the whipped cream. Fold in half the whites just until incorporated, then fold in the remaining whites, and finally the remaining whipped cream. Refrigerate for at least 8 hours.

4-1/2 oz. bittersweet chocolate, finely chopped
2 Tbsp. (1 oz) unsalted butter, diced
2 Tbsp. espresso or very strong coffee
1 cup chilled heavy cream
3 large eggs, separated
1 Tbsp. sugar

## Hazelnut Sauce:

Put hazelnuts in an 8- or 9-inch pan. Bake in a 350° oven until the nuts are golden under skins, about 15 to 20 minutes. Pour onto a clean towel and, when cool enough to touch, rub nuts with fabric to loosen skins. Lift nuts from towel; discard skins. Coarsely chop nuts.

In a 10- to 12-inch nonstick frying pan over high heat, combine sugar and butter. Shake pan frequently to mix until sugar and butter are melted and amber colored, about 5 minutes; watch carefully.

Off the heat, add whipping cream (the mixture will foam); stir until caramel is smoothly mixed with cream. Stir in chopped nuts and liqueur.

Return sauce to medium heat and stir until boiling vigorously, about 6 minutes. The sauce can be served hot or cold.

Chop the remainder of hazelnuts and hold for service.

1/2 cup and 1 Tbsp. hazelnuts
3/4 cup sugar
3 Tbsp. butter or margarine, cut into chunks
1/2 cup whipping cream
1/4 cup hazelnut-flavor liqueur

## Assembly:

Pipe layers of Peanut Butter Mousse and Chocolate Mousse into 3-oz glasses. Drizzle Hazelnut Sauce over then repeat the layers of mousse. Top with Hazelnut Sauce and chopped hazelnuts.

**Chef Eric LeVine** is a Food Network Chopped champion and a partner in Morris Tap and Grill in Randolph, NJ. He is the author of *Small Bites Big Flavor: Simple, Savory and Sophisticated Recipes for Entertaining*

*Savoring the Shore*

# Choco Avo Mousse

*Linda M. Jensen, Nutritionist, Mary's Place by the Sea, Healing Arts Practitioner*

Mix first 4 ingredients in food processor until smooth. Fill phyllo cups (or dessert dishes) and garnish with a raspberry or strawberry slice and mint. Sprinkle with shredded coconut.

## Suggestions:

May be refrigerated, but not necessary

May be frozen for future use

*May be put into small dessert dishes for a totally raw dessert*

This recipe comes from **Linda M. Jensen,** the nutritionist for Mary's Place by the Sea which is a center for help and healing in Ocean Grove, NJ, for women and their families who are battling cancer. Linda is a certified cancer support and nutritional educator and a healing arts practitioner in Rumson, NJ. She is the author of *"Survolve, Small Changes, Big Results."*

1/2 cup carob powder

2 avocado, ripe, peeled and pit removed (you would be surprised as to how many ask!)

1/2 cup almond or cashew butter

4 Tbsp. raw agave, or brown rice syrup or 2 Tbsp. honey

*Optional* 1 package phyllo dough cups, premade*

Fresh raspberries or sliced strawberries for garnish

Shredded raw coconut and mint for garnish

# Aloha Chocolate Mousse

*Chef Marilyn Schlossbach, Langosta Lounge, Asbury Park, NJ*

*"On a self-imposed birthday trip to Maui for some alone time at Swell Women's Surf and Yoga Retreat. I am not a raw food person but this recipe blew my flip flops off...."*
*– Chef Marilyn Schlossbach*

Scoop out avocados. Put all ingredients in the food processor and blend until very smooth

6 avocados

1-3/4 cup agave

1-1/2 cup cocoa

1/2 cup palm or coconut oil

1/4 Tbsp. cinnamon

1/2 tsp. nutmeg

2 Tbsp. vanilla

**Chef Marilyn Schlossbach** has been named one of the Best Chefs America 2013. She owns a number of restaurants at the NJ Shore including Langosta Lounge, Asbury Park NJ.

*Savoring the Shore*

# Maple Custard

*Jessica Mariconda*

3 eggs
1/2 cup of maple syrup
2 cups milk
Pinch of salt

Pre-heat oven to 325 degrees F. Mix all the ingredients into a large bowl. Pour into custard dishes

Place custard dishes in a pan of water. Bake for 45 minutes – 1 hour.

# The WGirls Seashore Surprise

*WGirls Coastal NJ, Red Bank*

4 – 3 oz. boxes French vanilla Jello brand pudding mix
7 oz. crushed graham crackers (we used 1/2 box Honey Maid Graham Crackers)
6 cups cold whole milk
14 oz. Swedish fish or other gummy sea creatures

Using either a food processor or hands crush graham crackers until they are coarse in texture.

In a large bowl, mix all of the pudding mix with the cold milk. Whisk together for approximately 3 – 5 minutes until the mixture develops into a pudding-like consistency. Use either a trifle bowl or a large decorative bowl. Spoon pudding into the bowl, and then spoon crushed graham crackers over top.

Layer a couple of Swedish fish or gummies on top of the graham crackers. Repeat layering the pudding, graham crackers and gummies.

Serve and enjoy!

*"WGirls Coastal NJ is an organization that provides underprivileged women and children in local communities, and in times of crisis at the Jersey Shore, with the support and resources necessary to achieve health, happiness and the ability to lead productive and successful lives. The members of WGirls Coastal NJ have a tremendous respect for the beautiful beaches and environment at the Jersey Shore, so they created this dessert to celebrate the oft-forgotten beauty and memories they have created here." – WGirls Coastal NJ*

*(Photo courtesy WGirls Coastal NJ)*

# Index

Index